THIEVES IN THE TEMPLE

THIEVES
IN THE
TEMPLE

The Christian Church
and the Selling of the
American Soul

G. JEFFREY MACDONALD

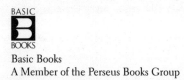

Basic Books
A Member of the Perseus Books Group

Books published by Basic Books are available at special discounts for bulk purchases in the
United States by corporations, institutions, and other organizations. For more information,
please contact the Special Markets Department at the Perseus Books Group, 2300 Chestnut
Street, Suite 200, Philadelphia, PA 19103, or call (800) 810–4145, ext. 5000, or e-mail
special.markets@perseusbooks.com.

Designed by *BackStory Design*
Set in 11.75 point Adobe Garamond by the Perseus Books Group

Cataloging-in-Publication data for this book is available from the Library of Congress
ISBN-13: 978-0-465-00932-9
10 9 8 7 6 5 4 3 2 1

To My Mother and Father

CONTENTS

INTRODUCTION

In 2002, the Community Church of Joy in Glendale, Arizona, was rapidly expanding. Construction crews were developing roads, a school, and other new buildings on the church's vast 187-acre campus. Administrators counted 12,000 names on the membership rolls and saw about half of them in worship on an average weekend. Professional musicians played through a top-notch sound system every Sunday, helping earn the church a reputation across the greater Phoenix area as a place for fun, upbeat relief from the daily grind. The congregation was lively, worshippers were happy, and Glendale's Church of Joy was the envy of its fellow southwestern churches.

Even while the church exhibited signs of success, senior pastor Walt Kallestad was having difficulty sleeping. The Phoenix metropolitan area displayed signs of trouble. Rates of crime, alcoholism, divorce, and unwanted pregnancies were steadily climbing. Yet attendees at the Community Church of Joy seemed oblivious to the city's social problems, as if they were happily separate from the rest of the population. Recalling Jesus' summons to care for society's most vulnerable, Kallestad asked himself disturbing questions such as, if our congregation disappeared, would the larger community even miss us or know we were gone? He knew his congregants weren't taking up their crosses and following a hard road of discipleship in their private lives. Reflecting on their behavior in church, he said, "They didn't really want to engage with God. They wanted relief and inspiration." His church had become a formidable institution, yet it had failed to address its neighbors' trials, or to bring out the best in its members.

After twenty years in ministry and a track record of celebrated accomplishments, Kallestad went before his gathered flock and tearfully repented. On his watch, he said, the church had become a "dispenser of religious goods and services." From now on, for the sake of God, church integrity, and society, life inside his congregation would have to change in a big way.

Kallestad purged frills churchwide. Gone were the talented professional musicians who had no personal passion for the faith. Churchgoers bid adieu to group trips to favorite restaurants, square-dancing classes, and card-playing evenings that had nothing to do with Christianity. Rebellion quickly followed. One out of every three members and about half the staff quit the church in protest. Members who remained were expected to practice regular devotions, tithe to charities, and serve alongside poor neighbors.

Six years later, the congregation still hadn't recovered even one-fourth of its lost members. But the remnant had learned important lessons: faith is costly, and spiritual growth involves sacrifice. "I tell people every week, 'If you're a spectator and a

consumer in here, then you are living in disobedience to God,'"
Kallestad says. "'And it's time you grow up.'"

The Community Church of Joy is reckoning with a spiritual
crisis that congregations across America have largely opted to
ignore. Faith has become a consumer commodity in America.
People shop for congregations that make them feel comfortable
rather than spiritually challenged. They steer clear of formal
commitments to Christian communities. They flee when they
are not quickly gratified or when they encounter interpersonal
problems. Changing churches has become as routine as changing jobs. As a result, churches are no longer able to help people
develop solid moral characters.

Religious mobility has become a way of life in America. In
1955, only 4 percent of Americans had switched religious affiliations in their lifetimes. By 1985, it was one in three. By 2008,
the number had reached a whopping 44 percent. Among
Protestants, including former Catholics, most people who have
changed their religious affiliations have done so because they
found a spiritual pathway or community that they liked better.
These patterns herald the arrival of a new religious marketplace, where churches overtly compete for customers and unsatisfied souls dabble to a degree that would have been
unthinkable just a few decades ago.

Though the trend of increasing religious mobility has been
remarked upon in recent years, news organizations have cate-
gorically failed to identify why it matters. They've focused on

which groups are growing, which are shrinking, and what all of it means for electoral politics.

The far more important question is, what does all this restlessness mean for spiritual development and character formation in America?

Though American society has seen a certain amount of religious mobility in prior generations, it has never before known such a competitive religious marketplace. Americans find options galore on a religious landscape that's grown exponentially more diverse over the past three decades. Church hopping is now so commonplace that congregations vie to attract and retain fickle attendees. Can churches that are aiming to please still mold people of high caliber? The answer to that question will have implications for every part of American society, from the Little League field to the office to the courthouse. Americans expect and need their Christian neighbors to be people who do what's right, even when it's difficult. This book explores the tragedy that results when new market forces steer American churches away from their essential, character-shaping missions.

I approach the subject first as a national reporter specializing in religion. I've been covering trends in church life for more than a decade, and my interviews with dozens of church leaders, parishioners, and expert observers over the years have convinced me that churches are becoming less effective in critical areas as they become more consumer-sensitive.

I also witnessed troubling dynamics from my vantage as the pastor of Union Congregational Church, a United Church of

Christ congregation of seventy-five members in Amesbury, Massachusetts. During my tenure there from September 2000 through August 2004, I tried to encourage meaningful discipleship commitments but found my efforts thwarted more often than not by a consumer mind-set.

Perhaps most importantly, I face this issue as an ordinary American Christian. I remain an attendee of worship services and a seeker of spiritual guidance from the Christian Church, an institution that I trust to be wiser than any one person. Its wisdom, I find, is increasingly elusive in an environment where pressures to provide lesser goods tend to prevail.

In all these roles, I've found that today's religious marketplace obscures a basic truth: the Church isn't a business. Unlike commercial enterprises that sell widgets or life insurance, the Church doesn't exist to satisfy the wants of customers. The Church needs to serve the higher purpose of *transforming* what its "customers" want, of diminishing certain primitive desires while cultivating holier ones. People need the Church to help them rise above their lower natures and come to care deeply about higher things, such as the well-being of a stranger in need, or the redemption of a hardened criminal. Our society depends on this elevating force to produce people who offer a conscientious compass in public discourse. But this force is rendered impotent in today's religious marketplace, where churches must either satisfy demand or go out of business.

Economic realities have come to imperil what the Church is fundamentally about: saving souls. This loaded and often-misunderstood phrase cries out for definition. The soul is the seat of the emotions. It's where desires for good and ill alike get hatched. Hence, a person whose soul has been saved through faith in Jesus Christ has different desires than a person whose soul has not been saved. Salvation is not about reciting magic phrases or doing everything to the letter of Old Testament law. To be saved by grace is to be freed to let go of destructive desires and replace them with passion for the ways of God.

When true to its mission of saving souls, the Church helps new desires take root. These new desires, when nourished, give rise to new resolve: a changed will, or "heart" for doing what's good. Whatever else churches do, from running soup kitchens to lobbying for public policies, should signal that saved souls are learning to love God and neighbor more than self. When the Church's capacity to transform desires is undermined, the Church abdicates its mission and functions just like any other customer-pleasing business.

If the Church fails to instill lofty values in Christians, no other institution on the American cultural landscape will fill the gap. Public schools, along with many of the country's most prestigious private ones, have nothing to say about what students ought to want for themselves, their families, or their communities. These schools try to equip students to reach their goals, but most dare not suggest what those goals should be. Similarly, mainstream media outlets don't strive to foster virtue. Local news shows are too busy generating fear of strangers and whipping up consumer appetites for new gadgets to worry about how they're impacting moral character for the worse. Cultural institutions such as museums hope to edify their clientele with stimulating exhibits, but they don't actively engage people in bids to make them, say, less materialistic or more patient. In the most important project of all—that is, stretching individuals to care deeply about the highest things—the Church is on its own. If the Church becomes unable to do that job, there will be no large institution in American society capable of shaping good people from one generation to the next.

The Church's present crisis reflects a rare moment in Scripture where Jesus shows anger. He's just arrived in Jerusalem, where crowds hail Him as a prophet, to find that the holy city's temple courtyard has literally become a marketplace. Money changers have set up shop. Customers come to trade. Each group uses the temple as a place to satisfy earthly desires, rather than as a place to surrender to God.

Aghast to see sacred space co-opted for personal gain, Jesus explodes. He flips seats and overturns the money changers' tables. One can imagine the traders' rage at having their coins thrown about and mixed in with their competitors'. Chief priests and scribes, who have permitted the marketplace to flourish, are indignant at Jesus' nerve. But Jesus stands His ground. He invokes the words of Isaiah and Jeremiah, prophets who had little patience for those who willfully violated the commandments and then sought refuge in the temple: "It is written, 'My house shall be called a house of prayer'; but you are making it a den of thieves" (Matthew 21:13).

As in Jesus' time, buyers and sellers in today's religious marketplace bear mutual culpability for betraying the Church's mission—any business transaction needs at least two parties. Both pastors and congregants have earned the moniker "thieves," since they effectively steal from God by leading His institution and His people astray. Still, it's worth remembering that even Jesus' angriest moment leads not to destruction but to restoration. As soon as He's said His piece, the blind and lame come to Him in the temple and are healed. I can only hope that some type of restoration will flow from my examination of mission drift in today's Church.

Although critiques levied in this book might apply to more than one religious tradition, I've focused primarily on American Protestantism for practical reasons. The probe would be too diffuse if I were to attempt an analysis of the entire religious landscape. Further, I know Protestantism from the inside, and this gives me insight that I wouldn't have in a more broadly framed inquiry. On its own merits, Protestantism is arguably the best laboratory in which to consider the effects of market-driven religion. Protestant churches are especially sensitive to market forces as a function of their relatively decentralized structures, empowered laity, and traditions of trying to adapt to the cultures around them. Protestantism also merits a close look because it's still America's largest religious tradition, with more than 100 million adherents. If American Protestantism loses its power to elevate souls, then a primary source of moral leadership in the nation and the world will be lost. The sheer size of American Protestantism means that a sea change in its character-shaping dynamics is important for all Americans to understand.

Also for practicality, I use the term *the Church* to refer to the established institution in its many forms. I'm not talking about a building. I'm talking about the many resources that exist to advance God's soul-saving mission (e.g., professional staff, volunteers, programs, and so on). I realize that this use of the term could generate confusion among readers who might insist that *the Church* be understood in its pure sense—not as an institution or a building but as a community of believers. I ask that purists bear with me as I use *the Church* in this less-than-pure sense in order to distinguish the institution from its clientele.

In the new religious marketplace, does the Church offer Americans a way to the highest things or yet another space in which to be self-indulgent? For me, no issue is more important than this one. I cherish the idea of the Church community as a distinct people, called by the Holy Spirit to follow Jesus, to live counterculturally, to bear witness, to make sacrifices, and to change the world for the better as agents of God's love. I can't stand to see the Church reduced to an instrument that strokes worshippers' egos and reinforces destructive habits of the heart.

When I think about the future of the Church, I think of my young nieces and the two young boys who regard me as a step-father figure. They need the Church, every bit as much as I did, to help them see the purpose of life beyond accumulating possessions, collecting accolades from admirers, and having a good time. Their lives can be rich in meaning, purpose, and satisfaction if the Church teaches them to care more about the well-being of their neighbor than they do about their own natural impulses to feel dominant, maximally safe, and ever more comfortable. They, along with the rest of us, need a wisdom that's not learned by simply observing nature, where strong species devour weak ones, or by reading inspirational literature or even Scripture, since we're all prone to hearing only what we want to hear. America needs the Church to be the elevating influence that God intends for it to be. Our job, however tough, is to make that happen, even in the age of the new religious marketplace.

PART ONE

CHAPTER 1

The Rise of the Consumer-Driven Church

HARLAN BRANDON, A MIDDLE-AGED AFRICAN AMERICAN businessman, still goes to church in the same part of Brooklyn where he grew up. But church for him is nothing like it used to be.

"There's been a big change," he told me as we sat together at a table overlooking the lobby and shops in the 120,000-square-foot Christian Cultural Center (CCC).

Some forty years ago, when Brandon was a child living in poverty, he heard much from the pulpit about humility as an essential tool for keeping the Devil at bay. Today in church, he hears practical advice for succeeding in business and improving his position in society. His preacher is A. R. Bernard, a former banker who attracts 10,000 congregants on a typical Sunday to his campus on Flatlands Avenue. Reverend Bernard's church is lavish in every respect, from the cushioned theater-style seating to the professional-quality band that plays during services, from the three giant projection screens to the singers in matching charcoal suits. "There's no way you can equate God with poverty," Reverend Bernard claims, adding that biblical images of Heaven feature gold streets and other signs of opulence. His church is a monument to his gospel of prosperity.

When the seeds of the CCC took root in 1981, the church was a storefront congregation in Brooklyn's Greenpoint neighborhood. Now, the community occupies a $28 million building, has a $15 million annual budget, and counts more than 30,000 members. That makes it New York City's largest church, attracting middle- and upper-middle-class African American professionals from as far away as Delaware and Rhode Island.

The gospel of prosperity is one reason that the CCC is flourishing while many other churches are floundering. "Jesus said, 'seek first the kingdom of God, and all these things will be added to you'," Bernard told me when I interviewed him in his spacious office, which features a full bathroom and a flatscreen TV. "The idea is that if you can abandon materialism and put God first in your life, then he will give you that materialism back so that you can do something with it." When he preaches in a dark suit from behind a glass lectern, listeners whip out laptops to take notes on how to be successful and get ahead in corporate America.

Remember: as creatures of God, you are infinitely valuable, Bernard tells them. God wants to "lavish" blessings on His people, he says, and we should help Him do it. Hatch big dreams, keep smart company, be a good listener, and use what you learn from those smarter than you. To get ahead in life, Bernard urges, be an asset to big business, not a thorn in its side. Listeners soak up Bernard's tips and praise, shouting "Bless you!" and "Amen!" in response.

The CCC is not alone in swelling its ranks by preaching prosperity. Mega-ministries around the country have blossomed by professing that discipleship is a ticket to wealth. Millions of Christians learn the life of faith from the likes of Kenneth Copeland Ministries, an institution that proclaims: "health and wealth belong to the believer." Or, as Kenneth's wife, Gloria Copeland, told attendees of a convention in Fort Worth in 2009: "God knows where the money is, and He knows how to get the money to you." Joel Osteen, whose 47,000-member Lakewood Church in Houston is the nation's largest church, pledges that "God intends for each of us to experience the abundant life." He assures donors that "because of your generosity, God's favor and goodness become a part of your life too."

Georgia preacher Creflo Dollar goes so far as to offer an online "School of Prosperity," where teachings from his vast, multimedia ministry get boiled down to practical basics. "Having no increase renders you useless to the kingdom of God," says the aptly named Pastor Dollar on his ministry's Web site. The School of Prosperity is "designed to teach you how to fulfill your God-given destiny ... by being His distribution center."

Prosperity preaching is a symptom of a deeper problem. Ministries of all sizes are packaging the Christian life as a consumer commodity, a customizable experience. This has become abundantly clear in the success of Christian retailing, a $4.6 billion industry that flourishes by equating discipleship with the joy of consumption. Pastor Rick Warren's best seller *The Purpose-Driven Life* has spawned more than a dozen spin-off items, from journals to meditations and DVDs, as readers snap up "essential" accessories for their religious journeys. Organizers of the traveling Christian women's conference Women of Faith tell women they can hear fabulous music, listen to hilarious stories, and "encounter a love that is life-changing"—if only they'll pay $89 each for admission ($109 for premium seats). When big Christian films such as *The Passion of the Christ* come to town, local church groups characterize moviegoing as an act of Christian witness. For those with a few dollars to spend, being a Christian has apparently never been easier.

Christian life hasn't always been so cushy. Jesus Christ himself lived as a homeless wanderer, with "no place to lay his head" (Luke 9:58). He professed that a rich man must renounce all worldly goods in order to enter the kingdom of Heaven (Mark 10:17-25). His earliest followers understood that sacrifice, sometimes even the ultimate sacrifice, was part and parcel to Christian life. Many of them died for their faith. Jesus made clear that the Church would be no place for anyone who wanted to minimize adversity or have an easy life in this world. "You will be arrested, persecuted, and killed," he tells his disciples on the eve of his death. "You will be hated all over the world because you are my followers" (Matthew 24:9).

The renunciation of worldly comforts remained a staple of Christian faith long after Jesus' death. Desert fathers and mothers of the second century, for instance, were seen as heroes for sacrificing food, sex, and even sleep for extended periods in order to master bodily impulses and thereby purify their hearts. Their practice was far more rigorous than what many worshippers could tolerate, but it established an ascetic ideal that would endure in the minds of Christians for centuries.

Sacrifice has until recently remained a central tenet of Christian life. For hundreds of years, monasteries and convents have trained men and women to live ascetically in order to better know the Lord who trusted not in worldly ways. Even after Protestants replaced the celibate priest with the faithfully married cleric, they continued to admire self-denial and tempered appetites. Think, for instance, of Methodists, who have perennially sought to keep their flocks sober; Baptists, who have discouraged the use of drugs, drinking, and even dancing because these practices diminish inhibitions; and Seventh-day Adventists, who commonly refuse meat as an act of discipleship.

Though the particulars of prior eras' ascetic practices often seem a bit silly to later generations, the understanding that an elevated heart stems from self-denial has endured—and still endures for many. But in the last three decades, America has witnessed a radical reformulation of the Christian ideal, in which the Church and other Christian organizations have begun repositioning the faith as a resource for satisfying primitive desires. How did we get to this point, where ministers expound and congregants seek a version of discipleship devoid of real sacrifice? It is a question that requires rigorous examination if we are to have any hope of saving Protestant Christianity in America from self-destruction.

AMERICAN SOIL has long been fertile for both religious individualism and religious innovation. Even before the Pilgrims landed at Plymouth Rock, they saw their quest in the New World as the response to a divine call. In this new land, they would strive to shake off Old World restraints and forge, in a freer environment, new communities where the Lord could be rightly worshipped and glorified. In this New World, they believed, they would not be bound to ceremonial, unscriptural traditions that gave rise to corrupt practices. They would instead claim power through grace to embrace a higher calling. To that end, they broke away from the Church of England and established a Christ-centered society—a "city upon a hill"—to serve as an inspirational model for the world to see.

The idea that an individual should take direct responsibility for the quality and content of his or her relationship with God became an early hallmark of American religion. It was on spectacular display during the First Great Awakening of the 1730s and '40s. Colonists flocked to hear George Whitefield, a traveling evangelist who brought grown men to their knees, weeping in repentance. By the thousands, they gathered in open fields, where the fiery Whitefield reminded them that no church hierarchy or membership would be sufficient to save their sinful souls. To be saved, each would need a personal conversion experience, led by the Holy Spirit and marked by overwhelming remorse, to be followed by the joy of being reborn in the Spirit. In a phenomenon unlike any seen in Europe, individuals across the colonies sought out the often-wrenching open-air experiences associated with personal salvation. In so doing, they demonstrated their conviction that no one save the Holy Spirit could deliver them into right relationship with God. Each individual would need to find his or her way to God's throne—even if that meant embracing expressions of faith that hadn't yet received official church approval.

By the late eighteenth century, Americans recognized religious individualism as an indispensable feature of their society. The landscape of faith had become relatively diverse, with Catholics, Jews, Quakers, and the Dutch Reformed, among other sects, expanding their ranks. Framers of the Constitution worried that state sponsorship of any church would threaten the Church's integrity, since governments tended to have their own agendas. They debated whether the new republic would be wise to forgo the type of state-funded church that they knew to be the norm across Europe. In the end, religious liberty prevailed. Freedom of religion for every American became part of the First Amendment in the Bill of Rights. Americans would forevermore have a right to seek God on their own terms.

In the absence of a state church, the United States developed a brisk religious marketplace. By 1833, every state had stopped funding churches. Without an inflow of government dollars, congregations were forced to rely on voluntary donations to keep their doors open. Competition for followers heated up. In some areas, especially less-settled ones, Methodists and Baptists aggressively maneuvered to attract new members. They routinely measured ministerial success in terms of the number of people baptized and sanctified each week. Members broke off to form new churches or to join new movements, such as Joseph Smith's Latter-day Saint movement, which later became Mormonism. The seeds of the exorbitant religious mobility of the current age were arguably sown in the age of the horse and buggy.

Today's religious consumerism, however, doesn't trace entirely to earlier centuries. Those who switched affiliations in the early nineteenth century had more pressing concerns than whether another church might offer more programming options or a more enjoyable worship format. Joseph Smith, for instance, left the church of his youth after concluding on his own that Presbyterianism wasn't "true"—i.e., its core doctrines didn't reflect God's way of salvation.

Sensing that God was ushering in the last days by unleashing religious freedom in the United States, fervent believers anticipated Christ's return by striving urgently to perfect their ways. Shakers established communes where they hoped Christ would find flawless faith and moral order. Activists for womens' rights framed gender equity in church and society as a necessary precursor to the Savior's arrival. On the frontier, Judgment Day seemed especially imminent and getting ready for it was the top priority. Methodism, which grew from a few dozen churches in 1776 to become America's largest denomination with 2.6 million members by 1850, attracted people concerned about their eternal destinies. Like Baptists of the period, Methodists drew followers who feared the fires of Hell and responded to preachers' urgent calls to repentance. The stakes seemed especially high—too high for a believer to stay in a church that was missing the mark.

As the twentieth century approached, the Church faced a very different challenge: collapsing faith. Rapid cultural change during the Industrial Revolution meant that Americans were often more concerned about securing their next meal than they were about securing a seat in Heaven. Church leaders realized that their institutions would need to offer something different than what they had offered to prior generations. An adaptable religious marketplace was beginning to emerge.

Intellectual trends put churches on the defensive. From Charles Darwin to Friedrich Nietzsche, Karl Marx to Sigmund Freud, many of the major thinkers of the late nineteenth and early twentieth centuries challenged the faith of Christians internationally. By the 1870s, scholarly biblical criticism, which contrasts scriptural accounts with those of other sources, had convinced many that the Bible bore the fingerprints of not-always-accurate human beings. The idea that the world was created a few thousand years ago in just six days, as Scripture seems to suggest, became increasingly difficult to reconcile with mounting geological evidence of a much older and naturally formed planet. Cultural anthropologists at the turn of the century criticized overseas missionaries—who had been considered heroes throughout much of the nineteenth century—for interfering with indigenous cultures. From all directions, it seemed, elite thinkers were at odds with foundational claims of Christianity. Washington Gladden was among the church leaders who worked diligently to keep up, authoring such telling titles as *Who Wrote the Bible?* and *How Much Is Left of the Old Doctrines?* in the 1890s.

Academics had support beyond the ivory tower as they turned away from religion. The popular media, too, began to critique religious culture. Cartoons in the humor magazine *Puck* (1871–1918), for instance, mocked Christians for engaging in colonial missionary work. One cartoon from 1895 shows American and British missionaries in top hats evangelizing a traditionally dressed Chinese man with sacks of military money by their sides. The caption reads: "According to the Ideas of Our Missionary Maniacs." Another from the same period depicts progressive and conservative missionaries choking each other in rowboats while indigenous people onshore hold up a sign: "We want no heaven. We want our ancestors."

Sometimes, the Church brought trouble on itself. The moralistic policy of Prohibition, enacted with support from Methodists, Baptists, and Presbyterians through the Anti-Saloon

League, became the laughingstock of the land. The 1925 Scopes Trial made believers in creationism look like ineducable fools. In its wake, evangelicals in particular retreated from the public square to forge their own separate communities of faith, distant from the rapidly secularizing mainstream culture.

As the moral authority of the Church began to wane, and as Americans increasingly turned to science rather than faith to explain the wonders of creation, church leaders realized that they would have to find new ways to keep congregants in the pews. To resolve this problem, they found their solution in the new spirit of consumerism.

In the wake of World War II, Americans became prolific consumers. A suburban building boom, fueled by returning GIs with growing families, created a surge in demand for labor-saving household appliances: washing machines, dishwashers with electric drying units, and plug-in vacuum cleaners, to name a few. Televisions became fixtures in middle-class households, revolutionizing how Americans lived and relaxed. Retailers mainstreamed the practice of selling on credit to a younger generation with more disposable income than their parents ever had. Ernest Dichter, an influential expert on motivation in the 1950s, coached pioneering advertisers to "give moral permission to have fun without guilt" and "offer absolution" for would-be consumers who still felt guilty about spending money on themselves. A pervasive consumer mind-set was taking hold on American culture.

Americans brought their enthusiasm for consumption to church as well. During the postwar period, the Church enjoyed a surge in popularity, partly due to the conformist and conservative spirit of the age. The percentage of Americans who self-identified as church members climbed from 49 in 1940 to 62 in 1956. Sunday-school attendance figures blossomed from 25 million in 1945 to 39 million in 1956.

New attendees had practical, often civic, reasons for flocking to church. In these anxious Cold War days, people looked to church as a place to plant roots, build social networks, and enjoy the comforts of a safe, collective refuge. Church attendance underscored one's pride in the American way of life, since American religiosity posed a sharp contrast to the avowed atheism of the Soviet Union. Lack of church affiliation could provoke questions about one's patriotism in a suspicious period marked by Congressman Joseph McCarthy's anti-Communist purge. At least partially for these reasons, a full 75 percent of Americans were church members in the 1950s. Representing a wide range of backgrounds, this generation looked to the Church to forgo potentially divisive rhetoric and instead bring people together around what seemed to be basic American values.

Like a customer-sensitive business, the Church responded to these particular demands by creating inoffensive, familiar environments beneath the steeple. In a wave of new church construction, planners designed understated buildings made from local materials to communicate a seamless blending of religion into the modern American landscape. Clergy sought a serene ambience for worship by advocating for stained glass, vaulted ceilings, welcoming foyers, and convenient parking. Flags had never before been a staple in American sanctuaries, but they became ubiquitous comforts near the cross during this patriotic era.

In terms of ministries, churches responded to demand for moral education as a means to reinforce values that would transcend religious differences. Even the teaching of doctrine came to emphasize how to think theologically, rather than what to believe, in a bid to smooth sectarian differences. The logic: Christians were bound to have disagreements, but they'd perhaps be more generous in spirit toward one another once they were educated on the issues. Political activism, a familiar feature of church life before Prohibition and again during the Great Depression, became virtually nonexistent in the late 1940s and early 1950s as churches sought to preserve harmony by avoiding all things potentially controversial. In these areas and others, the Church adjusted its game to suit contemporary desires in the pews. This led to some of the highest rates of church involvement of the twentieth century.

The Church also proved it could still grow numerically, even after enduring decades of doubt about its doctrinal teachings. Like hagglers in a market, church leaders and churchgoers had reached a deal. As long as no one demanded anything more than token sacrifice, parishioners would continue to support the institution, relying on it to serve any number of practical purposes in their lives.

In the 1960s, religious consumerism became more individualistic as Americans reexamined what role, if any, church life should play in their spiritual pursuits. Distrust of authorities and institutions of all stripes, including the Church, swelled under the shadow of an unpopular Vietnam War. The Church's close association with patriotic initiatives of the 1950s became something of a liability a decade later. Skeptics saw the institution as part of the cultural establishment, and therefore an impediment to social justice. Disillusioned clerics, who felt increasingly disrespected and alone in a culturally hostile environment, left secure church jobs in droves and sought satisfaction in other professions.

A rising generation challenged the near monopoly that Christianity had enjoyed in the spiritual lives of most Americans to that point. Americans, particularly the young, embarked on journeys of spiritual self-discovery, dabbling in world religions. Eastern religious practices enjoyed a sudden wave of popularity. Only 5,000 Americans had called themselves Baha'i in 1947, but by 1969 there were 440 local assemblies and members in 2,570 cities. Zen Buddhism garnered strong interest, especially on college campuses. Americans also sought spiritual enlightenment beyond conventional religion, through such avenues as astrology, nature-based practices, and psychedelic drugs. Practices derived from India, such as yoga and Transcendental Meditation, caught on as figures as prominent as the Beatles tracked down gurus and extolled their techniques.

Across the country, and in expatriate hubs from Marrakech to Katmandu, Americans were approaching religion for the first time as something to be sampled, critiqued, tailored to suit one's taste, or discarded if it failed to satisfy. The underlying impulse was not necessarily a shallow one: many of these pioneers were seeking a higher authority to replace the fallen human ones that had let them down. But too often these seekers confused feeling good with being spiritually enlightened. Having rejected the religious traditions of their youth, many had no accountability structures in their spiritual lives to point them toward anything higher than feelings of ecstasy. Their methods had at least one profound implication: in America, a life of faith would hereafter be understood as a journey, one that allows for moving on whenever one feels unsatisfied.

Denominations committed to ecumenism played down their differences and blessed the crossing of denominational lines. The Presbyterian Church in the United States in 1967 loosened its belief requirements to make the path to membership easier for people from other Christian backgrounds. The Episcopal Church began permitting its members in 1968 to accept Communion at non-Episcopal churches and to offer Communion to baptized members of non-Episcopal congregations. Churchgoers consequently experienced a wider swath of Christianity and found, as consumers are wont to do, that they liked some religious attitudes and practices better than others.

As the faithful experimented with new options, they became increasingly demanding, and insisted upon new ways of doing business within their home churches. For example, parishioners within mainline denominations insisted that their churches adapt to the modern world by ordaining women. Others called on church leaders to work for the passage of civil-rights legislation and to denounce the Vietnam War. Protestants drew inspiration from the Roman Catholic proceedings of Vatican II (1962–1965), in which a church more hierarchical than most in Protestantism nevertheless affirmed and expanded the roles of its laity. If laity could speak with power in Catholic circles, the reasoning went, then Protestants unencumbered by religious bureaucracy should certainly feel empowered to speak out.

The Church responded with surprising alacrity to its newly emboldened parishioners. In a seismic departure from centuries of scriptural interpretation, according to which only men were presumed acceptable church leaders, several mainline denominations began ordaining women in the 1960s and 1970s. These moves caused some controversy, but they also satisfied intense calls from the pews for the Church to set a bold example for gender equality in society. Mainline churches also indulged their clientele by revamping the practice of ministerial counseling. The modified version would involve principles appropriated from psychotherapy, such as mirroring and letting parishioners find their own answers instead of offering directive advice. In this era of skepticism toward authority, these changes in counseling techniques helped make parishioners more comfortable by bringing clergy down a notch from their positions of power.

In effect, God's representatives now presented themselves not as authorities but instead as companions for the journey, wherever it may lead. Meanwhile, "parachurch," or special-purpose, groups increasingly sprang up as independent organizations to work on particular causes. For example, the Society of Separationists formed in 1963 to keep conservative Christian values out of public life. One year later, the Bible Creation Association launched to promote creationism in public schools. By drawing supporters on the basis of personal interests rather than traditional ties to denominations, parachurch groups boomed. During the '60s and '70s, parachurch groups grew more than 30 percent faster than denominations did. On multiple fronts, the Church was responding once again to consumer demand, albeit of a very different type than that of a decade earlier.

By the mid-1970s, the self-directed approach to religion had morphed from a phenomenon of the hippie fringe to an emerging norm in American Protestantism. Not all denominations experienced these changes in the same way, of course, or at the same pace. Evangelical churches remained relatively impervious to religious consumerism during the '60s and early '70s—they repeatedly blocked minor efforts to ordain women and continued to emphasize winning converts over offering soothing pastoral care. But within a few years, they too would be affected by unprecedented consumerism during a cultural lurch toward social conservatism.

By the late 1970s, even Christian conservatives were approaching faith as a customizable consumer experience. Readers of a conservative bent made James Dobson's *Dare to Discipline*, a book on the merits of stern child rearing, into a cult classic. Christians incensed by *Roe v. Wade* connected with like-minded believers in organizations such as Jerry Falwell's Moral Majority, a coalition for political action. First-generation televangelists such as Jimmy Swaggart and Jim Bakker tapped a lucrative business model that involved delivering the sensation of old-time religion to millions who could now get all their churchly uplift without leaving their living rooms. Self-directed religion was becoming commonplace for conservatives as they flocked to churches where their values were affirmed and where they received no pressure to reconsider their lifestyles. Even those who hungered for discipline sought out habits that meshed with pre-existing personal goals, such as being cheery at all times. Tailoring faith experiences to suit personal tastes had become as much a reality in conservative Colorado Springs as it was in liberal San Francisco.

By the 1990s, the idea had become commonplace that parishioners were entitled to shop for the right "fit" when choosing a church. Guidebooks emerged to help the curious select a church or even a religion that matched their values and preferences. Scotty McLennan's *Finding Your Religion: When the Faith You Grew Up with Has Lost Its Meaning* told readers how to pick a faith, any faith, based on their "religious leanings." Readers were then encouraged to surround themselves with like-minded people. Barbara Stevenson's *Church Shopping in the Bay Area* helped "nonbelievers, seekers and others" find a fit by sorting churches on the basis of buzzwords and subtle clues. For example, "cultural creative" types got a list of thirteen local congregations where the "unofficial dress code is 'play clothes' casual" because that—along with the presence of female lead clergy and liturgical dance—supposedly indicated a congregation with progressive politics. "If you are wrestling with what you believe," Stevenson writes, "people who settled those questions a long time ago are probably not the best company for you." Relatedly, Stevenson urged readers to avoid congregations where many attendees have never switched denominations because they likely aren't committed to the perpetually "seeking" way of life. These books and other cultural phenomena reinforced the burgeoning assumption that finding God is supposed to be a lot like shopping for a club membership: it's all about fulfilling your wish list and feeling comfortable among like-minded people.

In this new environment, churchgoers could and did leave congregations (sometimes serially) for any number of reasons, among them uninspired preaching, conflict with fellow parishioners, or a desire to protest new policies or practices. Churchgoers learned to wield influence by voting, or threatening to vote, with their feet. They were in effect training organizations and church leaders to cater to their professed needs, even if their demands for new gym equipment or yoga classes weren't exactly essential to soul saving. Woe to the congregation that wouldn't take its marching orders from feedback cards dropped in the offering plate.

The meteoric rise of customer-driven religion in recent decades explains why churches increasingly look, sound, and act like

American corporations. They've adapted their forms and systems to be maximally efficient and responsive to shifts in the marketplace.

Prominent churches in the twenty-first century function as religious businesses. Some leaders, including Reverend Bernard, call themselves CEOs. Other members of the clergy have adopted titles that sound suspiciously corporate as well: pastor for administration, pastor for outreach, and so forth. Boards of deacons or trustees too often resemble corporate boards of directors, overseeing management and tracking attendance rather than focusing on the spiritual mission of the church. The organizational structures of large Protestant churches mirror the structure of the American corporation, which many church officials revere for its efficiency in recruiting and maintaining customers.

It's not just the biggest churches or the evangelical ones that are adapting their structures to a consumer-driven climate. Even in the small, mainline congregation where I was a pastor, governance committees consisted largely of businesspeople who brought to the church the skills and methods of their corporate lives. They called for more demographic research to enable targeted outreach and more aggressive fundraising based on secular formulas. They relied on parishioner surveys—with questions such as "What do you like most about Union Church?"—to chart the church's future course.

When I was seeking a ministry position, the chair of the committee that recruited me to Union Church was a professional headhunter in the corporate world. The church put on a presentation smooth enough to impress any executive. The committee met with me over hors d'oeuvres and iced tea at the headhunter's big new hilltop home, where we sat on wicker furniture on a four-season porch. When we visited the church for the first time, we rode together in the headhunter's plush Acura sedan and took the scenic route along the Merrimack River. All of this represented a living standard far above the norm of Union Church's working-class congregation. Years later, the headhunter and I shared a laugh when he admitted that he'd used all of his corporate tricks to make an impression that would blow me away. He'd wanted to be sure I wasn't scared off by a congregation so poor that it met in a modest building with peeling paint and didn't even have an office for the pastor.

In churches big and small, it seems, governing structures have come to mirror those of organizations that specialize in satisfying their "best" customers (read: those with the most to offer the institution in terms of donations and professional talents). Perhaps it was bound to happen eventually in a consumer-driven marketplace, but American society will be paying spiritual costs for this shift for years to come.

Megachurches, defined as those with at least 2,000 attendees on an average weekend, provide particularly salient examples of consumer-driven restructuring. They've blossomed in almost every region of the country in part by making churches feel like malls. Many of these churches come with Starbucks cafés, Subway restaurants, or bookstores. Just as cafés delight the senses of smell and taste, contemporary churches offer a feast for eyes and ears. Megachurches easily spend tens or even hundreds of thousands of dollars on video and sound systems because today's worshippers expect the best. In sermons, attendees gain practical knowledge for pursuing goals they already hold dear, such as advancing in their careers. In small groups, they find people with shared interests in anything from jogging to knitting because that gets people connected to one another and, by extension, to the institution. With church Web sites, e-mail lists, and social-networking tools, congregations make sure attendees stay connected. Churchgoers get lots of useful tips and information to enhance (almost never challenge or overhaul) their lifestyles, which are treated as if they are beyond reproach. The objective of many megachurches is in effect the objective of every other kind of business: to ensure that the customer is satisfied and that the institution is both profitable (or generating surplus, in nonprofit parlance) and growing numerically. In this context, the higher goods that Christianity has to offer, such as guidance in the cultivation of virtue, too often fall by the wayside.

THE CONSUMERIST APPROACH to religion has produced a spiritual crisis in America. To restore the Church as a character-shaping force, we must understand the dynamics of the new religious marketplace and find wiser ways to navigate it. The opportunity for ordinary worshippers to take control of their religious lives and their religious institutions has proven irresistible. The relationship between clergy and laity has been reversed—increasingly, congregants in the pews get to dictate which aspects of religious faith they will abide, and which they will ignore. Churchgoers no longer have to put up with components of religious life that they find distasteful, difficult, or less than gratifying in the short term. After centuries of subscribing to standards and codes that weren't always fun to follow, churchgoers feel liberated, like young adolescents who've been left home alone for the first time. The vacuum of authority has allowed parishioners to enjoy the spiritual equivalent of spending all day on the couch, eating cupcakes for dinner and watching sitcoms until the wee hours.

Customers in the new religious marketplace seem to have little awareness of what has been lost in the course of this transformation. Age-old ideas about what constitutes a "new heart" have been abandoned. Christians have long understood human desires as "disordered," as Augustine of Hippo says, until they get rectified through grace. This process allows for virtue to coalesce as a shield against primitive and destructive passions. In Martin Luther's rendering, "our will, principally because of its corruption, can do no good of itself … in a man who lacks the Spirit, nothing is left that can turn itself to good." The human condition, as Protestants understand it, means that churchgoers need consistent purging and strengthening of the heart, such that they might cultivate indomitable love for God's priorities and for their neighbors' well-being. But unless people are weaned on the writings of Augustine, Luther, and other wise Christian thinkers—and notably few are these days—they aren't likely to know just how disordered their desires really are, and thus how serious their spiritual needs are.

In the consumer-driven age, parishioners are not educated from the pulpit or elsewhere on what they ought to be demanding from the Church in terms of reordering their desires. In my experience working with parishioners and interviewing churchgoers, I haven't met anyone who's asked to bring his or her desires into fuller alignment with God's. Unless we openly address the competitive nature of the new religious marketplace, and educate our parishioners about what they *should* be demanding of their church experiences, we can expect religious consumers to keep demanding the cost-free approach to discipleship that has come to mark and mar our generation.

Convincing Americans to demand rigor in their church lives may involve facing down the demons of consumerism. American popular culture has helped give the consumer approach to religion its staying power. As early as the 1950s, successful advertising strategists such as Rosser Reeves were proving that people respond most effectively to sales pitches that appeal to their most primitive desires. Since then, marketers have convinced Americans to want whatever spares them discomfort. Advertisers hawk everything from weight-loss products to investment strategies by promising that there's no sacrifice required. No doubt consumer expectations have shaped marketing strategies as much as marketing strategies have shaped consumer expectations, and what has emerged is a population of Americans who are leery of *anything* that requires substantial personal cost. But a church without genuine spiritual discipline is as effective at elevating souls as a doughnut diet is at slimming waistlines.

The forces that have created this new religious marketplace are unlikely to abate. Consumer culture is simply too strong in America, as is the relentless individualism that makes many congregants suspicious of traditional church hierarchy. Nor do we necessarily *want* to turn the clock back. The American church sector remains financially strong, with donors giving about $100 billion to religious organizations each year. Clearly, many religious consumers are happy with the choices they're being offered. If the Church is going to survive in America, it will have to accommodate consumers' desires to some extent. The challenge will be to do so while offering useful guidance and direction that does more than pander to superficial customer demands.

America's unique religious history, marked by competition for souls, may help illuminate any latent genius lurking in today's deeply flawed religious marketplace. After all, it's on these shores—where churches don't survive if they don't attract supporters—that more than 40 percent of all residents say they've attended a worship service within the past week. That contrasts sharply with major European nations, where taxpayers still keep churches afloat and only about 20 percent of the population (sometimes less) attends church regularly. The teeming diversity of America's religious landscape has arguably been enhancing quests for God ever since zealots hot for converts first brought new brands of faith to the frontier. Perhaps now this varied landscape needs a bit more diversity as churches compete to extend grace at an ever-cheaper price. True spiritual discipline has become a rarity, and many purveyors seem convinced that the market for it has dried up. But they may be wrong. Americans may be hungrier than anyone has recognized in recent years for the kinds of challenges that turned their ancestors into spiritual giants. But first, a more immediate challenge looms: to make opportunities for character formation available in a marketplace that encourages anything but.

CHAPTER 2

On a Mission to Entertain

ONE SUNDAY MORNING IN SEPTEMBER 2007, I RECEIVED an invitation to get baptized by a church headed by one of America's most beloved church leaders: best-selling author Max Lucado. But I wasn't the only one chosen for this honor.

The setting was Oak Hills Church, Lucado's San Antonio megachurch, where an electronic marquee flashes worship times and uniformed police officers direct traffic. Inside, I was sitting in stands suitable for a high-school basketball game, waiting for the service to begin, when an assistant minister announced a list of upcoming fun events. The church was sponsoring a weekend getaway for young adults and a chili cook-off for anyone with an appetite. Topping the list was a baptism, occurring that afternoon, to which I—along with 800 of my fellow worshippers—was invited. All were welcome to watch this grandiose display of faith on the banks of the San Antonio River—or, as I later found out, to take the plunge ourselves.

"If you haven't seen it before, you need to know: IT—IS—AWESOME!" boomed the speaker at the podium. According to his description, believers would be gathered at the river's edge, just like the biblical masses who sought out John the Baptist. At 3 p.m., individuals would take turns professing faith, getting dunked, and resurfacing with joyful gestures and shouts of praise. He assured us it would be a must-see spectacle.

But few in the worshipping crowd seemed excited about it. During the announcement, parishioners talked among themselves, paying as much attention as frequent fliers do during pre-flight safety presentations. Maybe they already knew the event wouldn't be all that meaningful. That's what I discovered after worship when I inquired about how these events actually work.

"What would I need to do to be baptized today?" I asked prayer minister Jim Potts. After all, in the early church, baptism required three years of preparation, including long periods of fasting. Even in the mainline Lutheran church of my youth, previously unbaptized teenagers went through a two-year course before they could receive the sacrament. Surely, I thought, this flagship evangelical community wouldn't baptize just anyone without some measure of preparation.

"Just show up at three o'clock," he told me. "We'll be glad to do it."

"What if I've already been baptized?" I asked. According to Christian theology, baptism doesn't need repeating since it's a sign of God's all-sufficient saving grace. A second baptism would only be "necessary" if this church were to doubt the legitimacy of my initial baptism as an infant. In that case, they'd insist on hearing a valid testimony of faith before baptizing me. But none of that mattered. This church apparently just wanted to dunk as many of us as possible.

"That's okay," Potts said. "A lot of people get baptized more than once."

"Do I have to believe anything special?"

"Just that Jesus is your Lord and Savior," he said. "I always ask about that when I do a baptism. If the person says yes, then we go ahead and do it."

"And what will be expected of me afterward?"

"Just start coming to church!" he said. Based on the day's announcements, coming to church would apparently mean taking part in one fun activity after another—picnics, outings, movie nights, and so forth. Worship would be fun, too. On the day I visited, Lucado used a series of goofy slides to loosen up the crowd. Even when he gently urged listeners to be ambassadors for Christ, he insisted that bearing witness could be as easy as volunteering to take out the garbage or letting another driver claim a parking spot in a crowded lot. A lower standard for the Christian life would be difficult to imagine.

Church life in congregations such as Oak Hills Church reflects a disturbing national trend. The Church in America has changed its mission from elevating human desires to providing spiritually flavored entertainment. From dazzling video displays to mission trips that are largely tourism, from watered-down liturgies to weddings that worship couples rather than God, churches are doing whatever it takes to attract crowds. Pastors decide whether to jazz up or simply discard once-essential elements of church life based on their power to electrify; their power to edify or sanctify seems not to matter.

The tendency for churches to act as entertainment venues grows directly out of America's new, customer-driven religious marketplace. Churches increasingly need to please customers who expect direct satisfaction in every area of their life, including the religious sphere. This is an ominous development for a society that relies on the Church more than any other institution to mold the citizenry's highest values and aspirations.

It's not only newcomers to Christianity who are bringing consumerist values to bear on the institution—it's also people like Oak Hills attendee J. B. Gibbs. His parents were missionaries who raised their children in the mission fields of Brazil. Now, single and in his twenties, Gibbs goes to Oak Hills on Sundays in part because its fun environment and famous, good-humored preacher draw big crowds, which make it a good place to meet nice women. He's a regular at the church's young-adult singles group. "I just like being connected to others who are like me— who are my age, who believe what I believe," Gibbs told me after worship. In particular, he appreciates that nothing more is expected of him. He doesn't take part in service projects, for instance. On the Sunday I attended, he and his friends dropped nothing in the offering plate.

Pandering to an entertainment- and pleasure-seeking crowd undercuts the Church's true mission. Consumers of entertainment products don't expect to be led through difficult circumstances in preparation for greater challenges ahead, like the Hebrews who followed Moses in the wilderness for forty years. They expect an uplifting, satisfying experience when they sit down in church. If a church production ceases to deliver what they want, they pass judgment on the show and stop supporting the institution.

Overcoming this "entertain me" mind-set is difficult at Oak Hills, according to Pat Hile, a minister who organizes the church's small-group programming. "It's a challenge to move people out of a consumer mentality of 'how can you help me?' into one of 'how can I help others?'" Hile said. "People come here to get what they want instead of what they need."

When I asked Hile how Oak Hills overcomes that challenge, he answered: "Poorly."

When church serves as mere entertainment, it can never drive its audience to participate in experiences that aren't innately entertaining. But that's exactly what Christians need: to learn to love the seemingly unlovable and shun what is tempting but deadly.

Worship as entertainment is an inherently flawed model. But as long as it brings big numbers in the door, it will continue to increase in popularity among a segment of church leaders.

In an attempt to compete in a TiVo and Netflix world of instant gratification, churches are experimenting with a range of entertainment options to attract crowds both on Sundays and through the week.

Christian comedy shows offer a reliably clean alternative to the cruder fare at comedy clubs. Events in Texas, Maryland, and Southern California routinely draw upwards of 300 attendees to church venues. Membership in the Christian Comedy Association, a trade group for comics, climbed from 40 to 300 between 2002 and 2004.

To lure perennially church-averse teenage boys, violent video games have worked swimmingly. Dozens of churches offer kids a chance to play Microsoft's Halo, a game that involves killing members of a wayward sect called the Covenant. It's rated "M" for mature audiences, but pastors nonetheless use games like Halo as an incentive to pack youth-group meetings. For attracting enthusiastic crowds, repositioning the Church as an entertainment hub seems to rank among the most compelling options.

Church leaders insist that entertainment ministries open portals for spiritual growth. "We have to find something that these kids are interested in doing that doesn't involve drugs or alcohol or premarital sex," said David Drexler, youth director at Country Bible Church in Ashby, Minnesota, in a 2007 interview with the *New York Times*. He said that staging Halo games is "the most effective thing we've done" to recruit teens.

Recreational shopping has found a home in the Church as well. Megachurches are opening their doors to corporate sponsors offering product giveaways such as McDonald's salads and new Coca-Cola products, which worshippers have been known to sample after services at New Birth Missionary

Baptist Church in Lithonia, Georgia. At least four mega-churches went a step further in 2006 and 2007. They invited Chrysler to conduct free test drives on their properties and give away tickets to Patti LaBelle concerts to anyone who took the keys.

Some pastors defend the practice of shopping at church on the grounds that people need access to good products. That's the idea at Friendship-West Baptist Church, an 8,000-member Dallas megachurch that is building an amphitheater and an Inspotainment Center. In 2007, Chief Operating Officer Rickey Hill told religion reporters that his church invites corporate sponsors to set up and sell loans, among other products. If a business "lives up to our vision of community" by offering positive goods and services, Hill said, then it's welcome to do business in God's house.

Apparently some pastors believe entertainment is justified when it serves a good purpose, such as conveying a poignant message to a youth group or helping a family receive a long-awaited new car loan. To find fault with pro-entertainment attitudes is probably to court the ire of a large community of happy churchgoers in America. But the Church, its supporters, and American society are all paying high prices for confusing entertainment with the Church's true mission.

Entertainment has become central to the churchgoing experience. One can't show up for worship these days without finding that Sunday morning has come to feel a lot like Friday night.

The very architecture of American churches has changed. Churches built in the past twenty years rarely feature the stiff-backed pews of old, which once signaled to our forebears that something important was at hand and they should stay alert. Padded folding chairs are the norm for new churches, unless they have sufficient space and funds to install plush, theater-style seating.

Worshippers are as likely to see a big projection screen in the front of a church as they are to see a cross. In 2000, 39 percent of American Protestant churches had projection screens. By 2008, the percentage had reached 65. Casual dress is increasingly the norm as well—attire suitable for going to the movies is usually acceptable in church, too. In fact, the contemporary American church has so much in common with the Cineplex that hundreds of churches actually rent space in movie theaters. National CineMedia, a movie-theater chain, went from renting just three sites to congregations in 2002 to hosting more than 180 churches in 2008. These are just a few of the ways churches signal that they're ready to entertain. It's easy to see just how little is expected of those who attend services—just come, have a good time, and make a donation.

Unfortunately, a church that functions like a fun house cannot fulfill religion's central mission. The Church can't transform the desires of people it's trying to titillate. Entertaining services send the unhelpful message that churchgoers' desires are sacrosanct; surely they're not in dire need of reform.

Further, entertainment-based services featuring everything from dynamic graphics to Dolby surround sound divert money away from projects that could be transformational for all involved. For instance, every time a church spends $15,000 on an electronics upgrade, it forgoes an opportunity to build five cinder-block-and-cement homes for people living in makeshift shacks in Port-au-Prince, Haiti. Funding homes in Haiti would help hone the habit of finding joy in a magnanimous type of self-denial. In opting for the electronics upgrade, the church reinforces the self-centered desires of its parishioners, who are the only ones to benefit from the investment. That choice eliminates an opportunity—in Haiti or countless other settings—to increase churchgoers' capacity for compassion by allowing them to put others' needs before their own wants. Thus, habitual efforts to make the Church stronger by bolstering its entertaining features ironically make it weaker by systematically thwarting its core mission: to reform hearts.

On a broader scale, the Church diminishes its ability to shape desires when it ventures full bore into the entertainment business, by trading its moral authority for a shot at greater popularity. Consider the implications of creating a platform for Brad Stine, a leading Christian comic who's been headlining at Promise Keepers events—large gatherings of Christian men—since 2003. Stine makes his living largely by caricaturing liberals who have "created a nation of wusses," supposedly by being too merciful toward children and animals. He brings the house down with one-liners such as "the liberal's 'spiritual' experimentation … always results in the amazing discovery that he, the liberal himself, is God." Not all Christian comics are as snide as Stine, but he's apparently reached the top of his field because his belittling style is appreciated in many Christian circles.

Churches only belittle themselves when they provide a stage for self-described Christian comics who ignore the faith's principles in pursuit of cheap laughs. Even when the featured acts aren't especially rude, churches nevertheless lose respect when the public perceives them primarily as entertainment centers. A call for meaningful sacrifice in a time of crisis wouldn't get much consideration if it were to come from, say, an amusement park. Only an institution with a reputation for valuing self-restraint and for guiding souls to embrace the difficult moral high road can get a hearing when the need arises for inspired sacrifice. America has reached such a moment, but its churches are too busy entertaining to have a voice in the matter.

As the Church loses sight of its core mission, less-entertaining elements of church life are becoming endangered or lost altogether. Tools of the Church that were once essential to shaping hearts are virtually impotent. The tragic result is a Church where edification and wisdom passed down through the ages are now kept from individuals who seek them.

Pressure to make worship more appealing in liberal circles is depriving churchgoers of singing's spiritual benefits. Jazz vespers, or evening worship services, has become a staple in churches from Seattle to Cape May, New Jersey over the past two decades. The smooth sound may draw a crowd, but, as fine as the jazz may be, it routinely denies worshippers the opportunity to sing, since lyrics in jazz are either nonexistent or performed by a soloist. This is no small matter. Singing has long been critical to worship—it prepares the soul, loosening up the body and the spirit alike. This is why revivalist services in South Africa and elsewhere in the developing world devote an hour or more to collective song before the sermon begins. It's why believers from atheistic or agnostic backgrounds have told me time and again that they came to love God through the singing of hymns. Sermons without song can stimulate the brain, but the heart—which is the part that ultimately matters in the eyes of God—is more likely reached after listeners have had the disarming experience of raising their voices together in joyful praise. Such considerations seem to matter little in churches where jazz vespers is getting a tryout and a warm reception. To be sure, jazz junkies who might not otherwise be caught dead in church are showing up, and that's causing jazz churches to celebrate. But the Church is relinquishing an essential tool. And individuals who aspire to hear God's Word aren't learning how to tune themselves to His frequency.

Conservatives are just as prone as liberals to jettison important worship experiences in the quest to be entertaining. I experienced this firsthand one Sunday in 2008 when I visited Hope Community Church in Newburyport, Massachusetts. When time came to confess sins, I was startled when those around me started tapping their feet and rocking their hips. First the projection software launched a catchy tune. Then the words of Psalm 51, one of the most somber and contrite texts in the Bible, lit up the projection screen: "Against you, you alone, have I sinned / and done what is evil in your sight / so that you are justified in your sentence / and blameless when you pass judgment." Worshippers sang along, bobbed their heads, and otherwise had a good old time. Who knew repentance could be so much fun? This wasn't a unique case either. The church was using material from an electronic library that's licensed for mass distribution. Most likely, hundreds of churches groove to that same confession on a regular basis.

This is cause for serious concern. True spiritual growth requires true remorse—not just going through the motions—in order for an individual to move beyond destructive habits. That's because the soul often needs time to marinate in deep regret before the will is moved to pursue a costly, better way. Yet Americans seldom recognize their deep need for repentance since American culture offers precious few opportunities to admit guilt. Ours is not a culture that rewards contrition. Those who take responsibility for misdeeds often make headlines or lose lawsuits. If the Church strips confession of its somberness, then Americans won't have anywhere left where they can grapple seriously with their needs for repentance and remorse. Sins will increasingly go unacknowledged; amends will go unmade. As church leaders vie to make worship as entertaining as possible, time set aside for heartfelt contrition is vanishing from the experience of the faithful.

Even the important tradition of the collective offering is at risk in the modern Church's entertainment culture. Because nothing ruins a good show faster than a plea for donations, the Church's tradition of passing the plate is fast disappearing. Churches around the country are pioneering alternative ways of collecting money. All seem to share a common motive: to grow contributions while removing a collection experience that some find inconvenient or annoying. Increasingly common "giving kiosks," which look like ATMs, allow churchgoers to donate as discreetly as if they were making a cash withdrawal. Thousands of churches have established automatic debiting systems to take fixed amounts from individual bank accounts at regular intervals. Others, such as Emmaus Road Church in Seattle, simply remind worshippers to drop dollars in a receptacle on their way out. What matters in each case is maximizing collections through an efficient system that donors like. As churches figure out how best to achieve that goal in their local settings, offering plates collect dust in closets.

This quest for efficient cash collection misses the point of the offering as an act of worship. In the act of collection, a congregation makes a tangible gesture of gratitude to God. It is a group ritual, pooling individuals' funds and offering them as a single body united by the Holy Spirit. The ritual shores up several understandings: approaching God as a group is an essential part of Christian life; churchgoers make sacrifices together; believers give in response to God's blessings as an act of praise.

Taking up a collection can have practical effects in terms of spiritual growth. The act of giving together each week symbolically affirms the mutual commitments of community members to struggle side by side and support each other. Such shared struggles can produce family-like bonds. In practice, this can mean that churchgoers care that those who are grieving get comforted, for instance, or that shut-ins receive visits. But the communal demonstration of shared sacrifice is missing when individuals give (or don't give) in private. The unspoken message of private, highly efficient collection systems is that all that matters is that the church gets your money—how it happens is inconsequential. Pastors sometimes feel the loss. One told me: "Why would you rob people of the chance to make this life significant? That's what I would ask these churches that don't take up a collection."

Even weddings, which bring infrequent churchgoers into contact with clergy, are evolving to satisfy desires rather than elevate them. Couples in the new religious marketplace engage pastors much as they deal with caterers, florists, and photographers—that is, with wish lists to be fulfilled on their special day. Much of the time, in my experience as a pastor, couples would prefer nothing more than a customized celebration of themselves. One pair asked me, for instance, to provide them with the text of my sermon in advance so they could edit out any ideas or turns of phrase that didn't feel consistent with their views of marriage. Another insisted that the service include no prayers because the groom was an atheist and speaking to God wouldn't feel authentic to him. Other couples have petitioned me to use secular readings and pop music in lieu of Scripture and hymns because the former felt like a better reflection of who they are—as if the guests had gathered to worship the newlyweds rather than God.

Church leaders can of course say no to particular requests, as I routinely do, but we do so at our peril. Congregations and pastors often depend on revenues from wedding services to supplement tight budgets. Gaining a reputation as a stickler can put a church leader at odds with influential laypersons who believe the Church needs to function like a customer-sensitive business. Not all pastors will bow to such pressures; some may regard the scorn they incur as their necessary cross to bear. But the incessant drumbeat to keep wedding customers happy increases the likelihood that customers will eventually prevail.

Weddings underscore the growing chasm between the church's mission and its practice. These events could serve as an opportunity to push participants to subscribe to an agenda higher than their own. Conventions passed down over generations, such as traditional vows and other formulations, give people a chance to affirm symbolically their entry into an institution bigger than themselves. At the altar, couples need to show they understand that in marriage, personal preferences don't always prevail. But they often send the opposite message because the new religious marketplace lets them take control as customers if they so choose.

Too often, couples use their privileged position to shop around for a pastor who will ostensibly permit them to be the objects of worship for a day. The concrete values the Church has to offer, in terms of nurturing the humble character that leads to a successful marriage, remain unclaimed. And with each passing year, the Church's ability to do this essential ministry weakens due to disuse.

The spread of market-driven entertainment in the Church has diminished what people take away from even the most sacred elements of church life. Baptism is a good example. One of just two sacraments in Protestant churches (the other is the Lord's Supper), it is a fundamental sign and symbol of God's grace. But the power of this symbolism wanes when baptisms get revamped to serve as entertainment. Unfortunately, the watering down of baptism as a tool for shaping hearts isn't confined to the banks of the San Antonio, but is very much at work in the white clapboard churches of New England and in many locales in between.

Churches are exploiting baptismal practices, which vary from one tradition to the next, in ways that allow for maximum entertainment value. On one end of the spectrum, conservative proponents of adult-only baptism have a policy that permits them to deem prior baptisms illegitimate. This opens the door for high-energy baptism bonanzas involving lots of previously baptized adults. Events like the one I witnessed at San Antonio's Oak Hills Church occur at scores of other evangelical congregations.

On the other end of the spectrum, mainline Protestant churches take advantage of their more open theology, which permits infant baptism on the grounds that God's grace needs

no human consent or accompanying testimony to be effica-
cious. This policy, too, has been abused in an entertainment-
driven environment. I know because my denomination is well
positioned in the new religious marketplace to host families
who'd like their infants to be baptized but don't want to make
any sacrifices to lead a Christian life. They want a traditional,
entertaining, public event to officially welcome their new child.
They seek us out in part because the United Church of Christ
offers many attractive, classic sanctuary spaces for holding such
a special event. We also have a flexible polity that allows pastors
wide latitude for deciding whom to baptize and what to expect
(or not expect) from the soon-to-be-baptized and their families.
As a result, my clergy colleagues and I field scores of requests
from bargain hunters sniffing around the baptismal market for
low-cost fonts. Many pastors welcome the attention and hope
their low-cost services will keep the baptized and their families
coming back. But clergy admit that that's seldom the case. Instead, people get their baptism on the cheap, without even pon-
dering the costs of Christian life. The teaching moment that
baptism affords is lost.

Woe to the pastor who tries to raise the bar. I tried to
heighten reverence for baptism by encouraging prospective couples with a newborn to join the church, which would entail a
four-week class and a public profession of commitment. This, I
hoped, would reestablish roots for their own discipleship before
they promise in the ceremony to raise their child in the faith. I
might as well have been a Wal-mart manager announcing a 50

percent price increase on all merchandise. Couples routinely said "no, thanks" and called other local churches, who often jumped at the chance to host a special, highly visible event involving a cute young child.

When word got back to my parishioners that these couples had initially contacted me, several in my flock called me to the carpet for "turning away families." They worried aloud that I was passing judgment on some families as unworthy, perhaps too sinful, to be baptized. This charge made no sense: Christians baptize precisely because all human beings are sinful and need grace (symbolized by consecrated water) to wash them clean. I was trying to restore appreciation for baptism by framing it, as early Christians did, as a serious commitment. But my customers in the pews didn't see it that way. They wanted the entertaining baptismal shows to go on, and they blamed me for reducing the number of baptisms performed in the sanctuary. I stuck to my guns, but the battle cost me political capital within the church. In the process, I learned pastors need more than solid theological arguments to win against the idol of entertainment. They need customers who believe some things are still important enough to warrant a measure of sacrifice or delayed gratification.

To forfeit expectations surrounding baptism is to bury one of the Church's most precious instruments for stretching hearts in God's direction. In my denomination, pastors ask the parents of infants being baptized such questions as, will you encourage this child to renounce the powers of evil and to receive the freedom of new life in Christ? Do you promise, by the grace of God, to be Christ's disciple and to follow in the way of our Savior? Parents can't answer these questions with meaningful affirmation unless they've made personal faith commitments.

When a church insists on such commitments from parents of the soon-to-be-baptized, parents get a chance to grapple with what it means for them as adults to be disciples. These are eye-opening experiences. In new-member classes people talk, often for the first time in their adult lives, about why they think God gave them this life and the fears that keep them from following in Christ's radically loving and courageous way. New commitments, disciplines, and habits tend to follow these sessions, which people consistently cite as highlights of their church lives. But experiences with this level of depth and challenge don't materialize when churches wrongly suggest that baptism is a low-commitment occasion. Though baptism's efficacy endures as a function of God's grace, it ceases to be an occasion for soul-searching and a higher reckoning when the Church jettisons all meaningful expectations from the ritual. A key instrument for advancing the Church's mission is badly damaged.

The watering down of baptism makes it that much more important for other types of ministry to pick up the slack and challenge churchgoers to be more than passive consumers of spiritual services. But the pressure to entertain affects these aspects of worship as well.

Preaching, perhaps Protestantism's most defining feature, is increasingly hard to do with integrity and impact in the entertainment-seeking church. I know from experience. Parishioners told me, through a feedback committee as well as in casual conversation, exactly what they wanted from the pulpit. They appreciated short sermons (ten minutes is supposedly ideal), anecdotes from my day-to-day experiences, and lots of humor. Each week, they said, worshippers should be dismissed promptly after one hour of worship and leave with a glow that comes from knowing God loves them just as they are. The committee charged with maintaining good pastor-parish relations reminded me regularly how I was doing according to these benchmarks.

Preachers, however, have a higher calling. Their job amounts to more than taking orders like a waiter and making sure everyone's tastes are indulged. My mission in the pulpit was to proclaim God's Word in such a way that hearts might open toward God's ways and values. That would sometimes mean comforting the afflicted, or afflicting the comfortable, or convincing attendees of their capacities to live morally courageous lives. Yet I served at the pleasure of a small congregation of about forty worshippers on an average Sunday, and as a group they expressed no interest in such exhortation. They'd visit other churches and report how entertaining the sermons were elsewhere. Their message to me was clear: if I insisted on feeding them spiritual vegetables instead of the soul candy that they wanted, they would eventually find someone more accommodating to fill the pulpit. Or they'd switch to another church. This was the new religious marketplace at work, with empowered consumers demanding what they wanted. And it certainly wasn't helping to advance the cause of bold preaching.

One Sunday, I preached a sermon on fearing God, a theme in the seasonal readings for the day. I explored why Scripture says fear of God is the beginning of wisdom, and how "fear" might be understood today as respect for God's ways, including the codes in the Ten Commandments. A few parishioners were livid. "What do you mean we're supposed to fear God?" one said. "I'm not going to be afraid of God. I believe in a God who loves me no matter what." The debate could have been a healthy one, but it didn't work out that way. Parishioners I was used to seeing every Sunday in the pews changed their habits, staying away from church for weeks to make a point. They protested against what they thought was a theology at odds with an entertaining and happy worship. As long as entertainment value was to be their barometer for evaluating church, preaching on difficult topics would fall on deaf ears.

I'm not the only one who's felt pressure to keep it light and fun in the pulpit. At least one preaching expert warns that anyone who's not able to work a crowd into a boisterous mood should think twice about going into parish ministry. Recent books on preaching, such as Haddon Robinson and Craig Brian Larson's *The Art & Craft of Biblical Preaching*, dedicate entire sections to the use of humor. Celebrity preachers almost invariably have not only an easy rapport with their audiences but also a gift for getting them to chuckle, if not guffaw.

It goes without saying that no one likes dull sermons. The question is whether American churchgoers know what constitutes good, effective preaching in an age when everybody wants to be amused, mesmerized, and then some. Appreciation in the pews for preaching's higher purposes may not have mattered much back when Christians stayed put in one church for decades. Listeners then weren't making and breaking preachers' careers with their feedback cards and church-shopping habits. But it's crucial in an age when worshippers are constantly passing judgment and voting with their feet. In today's marketplace, an insightful, grounded preacher with a sober style may not last more than a couple of years—if he or she gets a pulpit at all. God help us when the only ones called to preach in America are soothsayers with wry wits, bright smiles, and good tans.

Missions, long associated with brave figures who spent their lives serving the destitute in distant lands, might seem a far cry from lighthearted entertainment. But the Church is reinventing missions in ways that make them more fun but less likely to challenge and elevate the values of participants.

Marketplace dynamics are pushing missions to evolve according to the needs of today's missionaries. Most noticeably, mission trips are getting shorter. Unlike traditional missionary activity, which required months of preparation and many difficult years in the field, short-term missions require only a few days or a couple of weeks away from home. Though cultural-sensitivity training remains as important as ever, today's missionaries sometimes spend only a few minutes reviewing a description of their destination before they fly. With expectations reduced, missionary activity is now open to just about everyone, and participation is booming. A whopping 1.6 million Americans did short-term missions abroad in 2005, and even more did them domestically. Smelling a brisk market, outfitters have launched businesses in the past decade to handle logistics and ensure that church groups have memorable, rewarding experiences. Whether a church group wants a week visiting orphanages in Russia or a few days wielding hammers and shovels in Central America, agencies stand ready to build the mission trip of a lifetime. An entire industry, with U.S. roots and overseas partners, has emerged to make sure American Christians get the exact adventures they want for themselves and their children.

This industry aims to deliver peak experiences for people such as Sam Massie of Boston. As a high-school junior in 2004, he traveled with his church youth group on a ten-day church-building trip to Honduras. But he knew early on that something wasn't right.

"It sort of felt like tourism," Massie said. "There was a sort of novelty to [working alongside poor people]. The focus of the trip was not enough on bringing benefits to the local place."

Massie explained why the situation felt weird. A group of skilled tradesmen from a remote village supervised, without pay, while these young Episcopalians tried their un-calloused hands at mixing concrete and laying bricks. The only local person earning a day's pay was an armed security detail, hired to keep the students safe from local threats. After seven days of roughing it at a local hotel with dirt floors, the group capped off its trip with three days of sightseeing in Tegucigalpa and three nights at one of the city's finest hotels. To Massie, the whole experience felt contrived. It gave the thirty-five kids on the trip exactly what their parents wanted them to have: a safe cross-cultural experience, a taste of outreach to help the world's poor, and a few days of tropical relaxation in high style. But Massie knew something was missing from a ministry designed with the missionaries' interests in mind.

Host communities have a compelling reason for accommodating just about anything missionaries want to do in their villages. They're getting paid for their pains. Payments from mission agencies to local communities abroad create opportunities for so-called vacationaries to work among indigenous people who can't afford to say no. This has repercussions for local economies. Even though local tradespersons need work in places from Tanzania to Ecuador, they routinely defer to less skilled American church groups who've paid for the opportunity to get their hands dirty and feel good about it. Customers in America's religious marketplace get what they want in the process, but they don't get to have their hearts stretched by listening to what communities really need from them and responding humbly.

Sometimes the religious marketplace inadvertently makes a mockery of missions. Children in one Tijuana, Mexico, neighborhood, for example, have learned to pretend they've never heard the Gospel as American church groups arrive every couple of weeks and shower them with treats along with messages about salvation. These weekend missionaries reportedly feel great about the souls they think they've saved. But a former trainer of church youth leaders near the California-Mexico border observes a different reality. "Each of these groups will come in, do a vacation Bible school, and lead the same kids to Christ over and over again," says Mark Oestreicher, formerly of Youth Specialties in El Cajon, California.

It turns out that missionaries are paying for opportunities to have a certain type of impact, one that conforms to their preconceived notions of what the world needs. But when hosts in impoverished communities simply play along to keep their funders happy, the new religious marketplace fails to advance the Church's higher purposes.

The competitive missions market is proving responsive to customer preferences. Organizers recognize that people want to work hard and play hard, too. In 2006, for instance, a group from Grace United Methodist Church in Alamogordo, New Mexico, made sure to include a Houston Astros baseball game in its post-Katrina house-gutting mission to New Orleans. In 2008, members of a youth group from New Hampshire's Portsmouth Christian Academy had as much adventure as service on a one-week mission trip to Belize. After leading three Bible-school sessions and helping assemble a small house, they were off to play: tubing down the Belize River, snorkeling at Thatch Caye, visiting Mayan ruins, shopping in an outdoor market, and attending "several awesome worship services, including a concert by the Afro-Caribbean musician, Mikal."

Outfitters craft mission trips as exotic and adventurous vacations in a bid to give clients what they want. They routinely promote their services as logistically "easy" and trips as "exciting"—as entertainment is supposed to be. Surely these outfitters would adapt if clients were to demand a different type of experience, such as one that responds more genuinely to local requests and makes a point to do sacrificial ministry on hosts' terms. But until customers demand something higher than experiences designed around their own desires, today's disturbing status quo is sure to endure.

For all its shortcomings, the contemporary missions landscape is not hopeless. Signs suggest that a discerning clientele might give rise to experiences that stretch missionaries' hearts and bless their hosts at the same time. For example, between 2003 and 2008, the Cleveland-based organization International Partners in Mission expanded its offerings of immersion-style programs from two to more than two dozen. These trips aim to deepen missionaries' faith by allowing them to experience how their hosts live, get to know their hosts on a personal basis, and resist the urge to fix immediately their hosts' material problems. Missionaries ideally return home from IPM trips with changed perspectives—and with hearts widened by compassion for people who face difficult challenges every day. Immersion-style offerings are increasing because people are demanding them, according to IPM director Joseph Cistone. This trend suggests that customer demands for church-based experiences can and do evolve—sometimes for the better.

When churches do mission trips through IPM, participants experience uncomfortable situations that test their convictions and evoke new concerns. One such trip brought about a dozen members of St. Paul's Episcopal Church in Richmond, Virginia, to El Salvador for a week in July 2008. Group activities intended to acquaint Americans with formative influences in Salvadorans' lives produced a lot of soul-searching inside sixteen-year-old Olivia Fabelo. A daughter of a Cuban immigrant, she'd grown up hearing that Che Guevara was a murderer responsible for hundreds of Cuban deaths. But in El Salvador, she heard story after story of gratitude for the Che-inspired rebel movement that swept the nation in the 1970s. Peasants, recalling those revolutionary times, told how his fighters had protected their villages during assaults and helped them become self-sufficient farmers capable of feeding themselves. Fabelo said the experience "was hard ... it challenged some of my deeply held beliefs." She defended her views, informing her friends on the trip about Che's darker side, but she also grew to have compassion and understanding for people she might have otherwise regarded as foes. Such a personally challenging process, she said, probably wouldn't have happened if she had spent her days working with her hands instead of listening, or if she'd been off sightseeing.

Even when deep personal convictions weren't being scrutinized, St. Paul's IPM trip was challenging participants to share in their hosts' pains and joys. Fabelo whiffed an unfamiliar stench of poverty when a Salvadoran teacher led the group through her school's neighborhood, a slum where everyone burned their garbage to avoid a city trash-collection fee. "I'd always cared about homeless people and poverty," she said, "but now I care more." Adults on the trip were also moved by what they heard and saw. Bruce Cruser, a fifty-five-year-old corrections administrator, nearly wept when a woman described how her entire village had been massacred during the revolution on a day when she'd been out of town. But he also beamed when he watched youth from St. Paul's play soccer with their Salvadoran peers in a pickup game, followed by conversations in which they shared what they hope to do when they grow up.

"That kind of thing doesn't happen when you're a tourist" or a missionary on a work crew, Cruser said. With a new concern for Salvadorans' circumstances, he hopes to return one day for a stint teaching English in a school he visited.

I do not mean to suggest that work-based trips are unnecessary, or that the "immersion-style" trips that IPM offers are inherently superior. Both can be done in ways that meet local needs and also stretch the hearts of missionaries. These IPM examples are important for illustrating how one agency has met both market demands and spiritual needs. By offering authentic encounters with indigenous populations and challenging customers on a spiritual level, this agency proves that indulging missionaries isn't the only way to thrive in the new religious marketplace.

The Church's current foray into the entertainment business could ultimately help the institution recall and reclaim its core values. By purging much of what churchgoers need for authentic discipleship, the entertainment-saturated church effectively dares its supporters to get proactive and demand access to well-trodden pathways that lead to real knowledge of God's ways. The question is whether churchgoers will lay claim to treasures stored away in their religious tradition or decide to remain content with cheap trinkets.

This experiment has shed light on an important reality: churchgoers value entertainment and probably always will. That's not a bad thing. I'm not proposing devotion to a dour or humorless spirituality. Even Jesus playfully turned water into wine at a Cana wedding, which suggests He knew something about when to kick back. But the Church must figure out an appropriate role for entertainment—perhaps as an occasional means of illustration or diversion, but not as the goal for congregational life that it has too often become. Identifying a proper role for entertainment in church life will be a critical step in recovering the Church's core mission of saving souls.

Christians in the twenty-first century will need to clarify how the Church will live out its mission—with or without an entertainment-based ministry. The goal of elevating hearts will remain an abstract ideal until the adoption of particular practices, structures, and systems makes it a reality. Today's obsession with spiritualized entertainment begs the question: do the Church's customers want anything more than to be entertained? As it turns out, they do—but much of what they're demanding is just as problematic.

CHAPTER 3

Church as Therapy

IN MAY 2008, HILLARY CLINTON AND BARACK OBAMA WERE battling for the Democratic presidential nomination. One of Clinton's most effective strategies was to attack her opponent for a heretofore unheard-of political infraction: being too committed to his church.

Obama's pastor, Jeremiah Wright, of the Trinity United Church of Christ in Chicago, was at the time gaining notoriety for his flair for controversy. He became a politically radioactive figure as clips of his sermons, including suggestions that the United States was responsible for the attacks of 9/11/01, started showing up on news shows and the Internet. Obama had close ties to Wright, who had officiated at his wedding and baptized both his daughters. Having attended Trinity regularly for twenty years, the presidential aspirant would find it tough to shake the stigma of his outspoken spiritual mentor.

Clinton's tactic took advantage of an unfortunate yet widely held assumption prevalent in the new religious marketplace. When people are offended by what they hear in church, they're supposed to quit the congregation and go elsewhere. When church becomes difficult or challenging, worshippers are expected to get up and walk away.

"He would not have been my pastor," Clinton told reporters from the *Pittsburgh Tribune-Review*. "You don't choose your family, but you choose what church you want to attend."

The press pounded Obama for failing to leave the church years earlier. Did he not regard Wright's views on American history, race, and foreign policy as offensive? If he did find them offensive, then why did he stay so long in the church? Obama insisted he hadn't been present for Wright's "incendiary" sermons and said he would have quit the church promptly if he had been. On the other hand, Clinton's assumptions about religious mobility drew virtually no criticism.

Underlying the episode was an understanding that religion is supposed to be comfortable. When church becomes a forum for ideas that don't dovetail with a worshipper's own values, that person supposedly has a right—even a duty—to quit the institution in protest. This premise, predicated on religious mobility and an assumed quest for the perfect religious "fit" with one's sensibilities, is so thoroughly ingrained in the American psyche that barely anyone thought to question it. After all, the thinking goes, no one in his right mind would attend a church that isn't perfectly attuned to his political views. But this mind-set reflects a deep misunderstanding of the Church's purpose.

The truth is, it's part of the Church's very mission to make people uncomfortable. Indeed, it must sometimes outright offend if it's going to be true to its purpose of transforming the way believers think and act.

Many of the Bible's major themes and principles are offensive. In the Sermon on the Mount, Jesus teaches His followers to love their enemies (Matthew 5:43–48). Yet to suggest, for instance, that crime victims and their family members ought to love perpetrators of horrendous deeds offends basic sensibilities. Jesus' prescription for resolving conflicts within the Church was similarly disquieting. When someone sins against you, He says, go and show him his fault. If he won't listen to you, bring the matter before one or two witnesses, or before the whole church community if necessary (Matthew 18:15–17). This kind of confrontation can be profoundly uncomfortable, yet only through such uncomfortable processes do people work through their animosity to find real peace. As long as the Church stays true to its message, some—including many of the Church's staunchest adherents—will initially take offense. If churchgoers regard their own discomfort as a cue to seek fulfillment elsewhere, then they effectively leave the table every time the meal is served.

God has been leading His people into unsettling situations in order to expand their hearts since long before the time of Jesus. Old Testament prophets from Amos to Zephaniah called people to abandon their indulgent ways and make sacrifices for higher purposes. Jonah spends three days in a whale's belly as payback for having fled when God summoned him to the unwelcome task of preaching repentance among his enemies in Nineveh. Isaiah proclaims, "Woe to those who are heroes at drinking wine and champions at mixing drinks, who acquit the guilty for a bribe, but deny justice to the innocent" (Isaiah 5:22–23). Amos warns the people of Israel to put away the songs and harps of their comforting ceremonies because they don't please the Lord, who seethes as His people trample the poor and flaunt their ill-gotten gains (Amos 2 and 5). Biblical situations time and again depict a people called to do what frightens them. God elevates through challenge.

With the advent of the consumer-driven Church, this truth has receded from view. The Church has taken pains to become comforting more than anything else, even though it used to be a simultaneously challenging and uplifting influence. As an alternative to entertainment, the Church increasingly offers comfort to make its customers happy. Preachers console even when situations beg them to hold parishioners to a higher standard. Small groups, organized around shared interests, offer indiscriminate affirmation rather than the rebuke or admonition that participants sometimes need.

Across the board, the Church is revamping practices to satisfy a clientele that demands self-help and therapy in spiritual packaging. In so doing, it is effectively renting out its character-building instruments to a customer base with other goals in mind. As a result, tools ordained to shape people into better versions of themselves are no longer available for their traditional purposes.

A certain type of comfort can be a strengthening influence. That's the case when the Holy Spirit, also known as the Comforter, comes upon Jesus' followers in the Book of Acts. Stephen is hauled before religious authorities on trumped-up charges, but he doesn't cower because the Spirit is upon him. He defends his faith in Christ, castigates his accusers for being hypocrites, and boldly accepts his fate as a martyr when they stone him. In instances like this, a comforting force can inspire brave, principled acts and the acceptance of personal costs for doing the right thing.

By contrast, the comfort demanded in today's Church too often serves an opposite purpose, that is, to soothe wounds and give refuge. This comfort shelters more than it strengthens. In excessive proportions, it encourages self-pity by showering attention on those who say they hurt. It coddles many who don't deserve perennial soothing but instead need to be toughened up. It feeds a church culture where just about everyone claims to be wounded, broken, or oppressed in some way, because victimhood is the ticket to the congregation's attention. This makes for a weak community because it doesn't hold people to high standards for courage. Such a community fails to claim its power to rise above such lowly natural impulses as self-pity. Mollifying comfort delivers just the opposite of the character shaping that the Church is meant to deliver.

To say the Church offers "therapy" is to use that term colloquially. True therapy would assist in curing diseases or disorders, including spiritual ones, such as greed or self-absorption. It would help cure the disordered heart, as God did for Augustine of Hippo, who prays: "It pleased you to transform all that was misshapen in me."

The "therapy" that today's churches offer is akin to what one gets from watching Oprah. This type of therapy might provide a morale boost, or shore up an attitude that helps someone cope. But it masks the need to reform what people want out of life. It glosses over ingrained habits of the heart, from gluttony to envy, pretending they're not as deadly as they truly are. This therapeutic function hampers the Church's mission by steering people to fulfill their lower appetites and to neglect higher mandates.

Between Sunday services, churchgoers often strive to live out their faith by leaning on one another to get through personal struggles. Ideally, believers offer one another strength and encouragement in the face of pressing challenges. But too often, churchgoers act as undiscerning cheerleaders when they gather in structured groups, where opportunities to challenge and improve one another disappear faster than the chips and pretzels.

American Christians flock in droves to small groups, where ten or fifteen people with shared interests or backgrounds routinely experience a type of therapeutic support. In the 1990s, more than one in every five Americans belonged to a religious small group. More than a decade later, the movement is still going strong. Members generally gather to discuss a topic of common interest, from Bible study to single parenting. Rules, whether explicit or unwritten, commonly reflect the sensibilities of 12-step groups, where emotionality is encouraged and criticism is unwelcome. When Christian small groups pray together, they focus on the stated needs of the gathered individuals. They say nary a word about wider moral or social issues such as war or poverty. So strong is the value of mutual supportiveness that an "anything goes" approach to spirituality almost always emerges, even among religious conservatives. A typical group ends up reassuring Joe in his divorce and Suzie in her bankruptcy that both are on the right track, even though what they may need to hear from friends is that they're giving up too quickly.

Research suggests that today's therapeutically oriented groups are failing to shape mature Christians. A 2004 survey probed the spiritual growth of attendees at Willow Creek Community Church, a South Barrington, Illinois, congregation that has been a model of market-savvy outreach and an inspiring trailblazer for thousands of churches that have launched small-group ministries. Results showed that churchgoers entered their groups craving to be challenged and held accountable to high moral standards, but this rarely happened. Instead, about 25 percent of all respondents reported being "stalled" in their spiritual growth. Many had become so frustrated they were considering leaving the church. This has implications beyond Willow

Creek because this iconic church has inspired so many others to create small-group ministries.

Willow Creek's formula assumes that churchgoers will become more committed if they join a small group of people who share their interests or are in the same stage of life. This approach has spread across the nation, and today churches of all stripes bank on intimate, small-group ties to keep people involved with the institution. Yet religious mobility is increasing with each passing decade, and the most common reason people give for switching churches is this: "the church was not helping me to develop spiritually." While small groups might offer members a sense of belonging, their therapeutic model is not challenging people enough to make real spiritual progress.

In fairness, there are small-group ministries that offer more challenging models. These illustrate the untapped potential of most small groups. In conservative circles, so-called accountability groups bring people (usually men) together to confess sins, examine missteps, and explore what might work better in the week ahead. Here the goal isn't to offer therapy or cozy comfort; it's to encourage a disciplined life consistent with God's ways and values. But this type of group has had limited appeal to date. Participants are often married evangelical men whose understandings of sin center narrowly on sex, gambling, and the use of intoxicants.

In more liberal circles, a select few groups embrace challenge by practicing group spiritual direction. In these sessions, participants relate recent experiences and let the group help discern how God's hand might be moving in their individual lives, even acknowledging when it is moving in unwanted directions. Once again, the goal isn't casual therapy or self-esteem building. The purpose is to recognize where God is leading, with help from individuals who've learned discernment techniques from such resources as the Shalem Institute for Spiritual Formation in Bethesda, Maryland. However, these groups are vastly outnumbered by those that take the easier path of universal affirmation.

Despite their shortcomings, small-group ministries are well positioned to play a major role in character formation. For starters, they're constantly adapting. Agendas are reformulated regularly. Participants, as voluntary attendees, are free to influence a group's goals and raise expectations for one another. No inherent obstacles prevent group leaders from challenging members to choose difficult paths. All that's missing is the will to turn small groups into teams that bring out the best in each member through strengthened faith, high standards, and hard work. But American Christians haven't yet used their clout in the new religious marketplace to that end.

Laypersons don't rely exclusively on one another for their religious therapy. Clergy also use their gifts and positions to offer comfort via counseling or pastoral care. In this they shy away from bolder traditions of pastoral advising and exhortation. Such methods are still needed, but they're largely unpracticed in a religious marketplace where churchgoers expect clergy to make them feel good about themselves and their choices—even when heaps of praise and consolation are unwarranted.

Today's pastoral counseling traces its roots to the ancient practice of "curing souls." Practitioners of this art through the ages would guide individuals to have experiences and make decisions that would allow them to enjoy righteousness through faith. This sometimes meant focusing on principles that reflect gratitude for one's salvation. For the guilty, they'd prescribe repentance and making amends. For the stingy, a regimen of charitable giving might be in order. Where faith hadn't yet taken root, clergy would plant seeds in one-on-one counseling sessions.

In colonial days, pastors used logic and persuasion to facilitate soul-saving conversions. In the early republic, when alcohol destroyed families, pastors counseled sobriety. Presbyterian elders made weekly house calls, encouraging people to take up habits that would help them resist temptation. Pastors-in-training studied the work of theologian Richard Baxter, who urged colleagues to "be ready to give advice to such as come to us with cases of conscience." By the late nineteenth century, pastors were counseling individuals to hone virtue in the public square by engaging in activities such as fighting to reform corrupt institutions. Issues and styles changed with generations, but the pastor's role of giving wise counsel to the morally conflicted endured.

Yet in recent decades, as parishioners expected the Church to provide secular-style counseling, pastors lost their ability to cajole and direct. Counselors in fields from psychology to social work generally refrain from giving advice, opting instead to let the other person chart a course that reflects her or his personal commitments. The pastorate has taken on some of the tendencies of counseling through the seminary. Mainline schools have adapted their training to suit denominations' demands and now teach techniques borrowed from psychology rather than the sterner medicine gleaned from ancient or even antebellum Christianity. Students learn to mirror feelings without judging. In clinical pastoral education, they serve as student chaplains in hospitals and other institutional settings, where they learn to listen, to advocate, and to bear witness to suffering. They also learn that they should not lead a non-believer to faith or counsel a hospitalized patient against cursing God. Such practices are seen as judgmental and inappropriate in clinical settings, and this perception has been transferred into the Church itself. As a result, laypersons have gotten their wish: clergy whose training reflects the modern world's professional standards. Pastors may still have a strong sense of what's right and wrong, but they've learned to keep such views largely to themselves.

Congregants lose access to valuable wisdom when leaders refrain from guiding or exhorting individuals in the ways of discipleship. This problem emerged in my congregation when a few teens were almost old enough to confirm their baptisms and become full church members. An educational committee decided that they should be mentored through the transition, but the panel refused to exercise judgment in picking mentors.

Instead, panelists insisted that each teen should choose his or her own mentor from the congregation, regardless of that person's passion or aptitude for the role.

The program flopped. One boy got discouraged and drifted away from congregational life after choosing a single, middle-aged woman who didn't want the role and resigned after a couple of meetings with him. Another boy chose a man who hadn't been baptized, had made no Christian commitments, and professed more confidence in Native American nature worship than in Christian doctrine. The lesson from this disaster was that judgment matters. Church leaders should have tapped wise and willing elders who would have proactively guided the teens to explore the costly, authentic ways of discipleship in adulthood. These giants in the faith might have shared personal stories to illustrate how and why they're willing to suffer at times for Christian values. Or they might have sought out a challenging mission activity to do with the teens. But none of that happened because, in this market-driven church, prevailing wisdom said that teens should set their own agendas and leaders should keep judgment and wisdom to themselves.

When churchgoers come to their pastor for comfort these days, many never get the challenge or admonition they need, and end up receiving comfort only. In my case, parishioners sought counsel primarily to deal with grief and sickness. My ministry colleagues reported similar experiences. Parishioners generally ask for help with managing the pains of grief, broken relationships, or chronic illness—and little else. To give that type of support is entirely appropriate, but it only scratches the surface of what pastors have to offer.

More than psychiatrists or therapists, clergy are concerned with the condition of the heart. They're attuned, for instance, to the emergence of bad habits that might squelch love of neighbor and hope for the future. Yet pastors usually aren't invited, as they were in prior centuries, to know the intimate details of congregants' lives. Nor are today's clergy trained to pry where they're not invited. Hence churchgoers get what they want in the short term: soothing comfort for coping with pain. They don't get the deeper analysis or the push to choose hard roads that they so often need.

Certainly, there are objections to this view. Some people resist the notion that pastors should challenge individuals to choose tough paths or give advice in moral dilemmas. They say clergy have no business making life more difficult than it already is and should confine their ministrations to comforting those in need. They also contend that giving advice is always counterproductive because individuals need to come up with their own solutions and learn from their mistakes. Alternatively, some people responsible for church budgets worry that a directive pastor could get sued for malpractice and expose the church to claims of negligent oversight. Others fear abuse of power. Departures from secular standards for counseling strike some as inherently "unprofessional," and therefore inadvisable. And some people simply like today's market-driven status quo, which effectively confines clergy to a sphere where all they dare offer in counseling is wishy-washy comfort.

Such concerns stem from one overarching worry: directive pastoral counseling might be riskier than an approach that aims to do nothing more than soothe. It probably is. But churches could manage liability and other risks with training that incorporates safeguards into the traditional art of curing souls. Pastors would learn when to push and when to hold back. This would still be riskier than the type of counseling that happens in today's world, where pastors are as engaging as wallflowers, but it would be worth it.

Christians follow a Savior who believed in taking risks. Leave your possessions and follow me, he told the rich young man in search of Heaven (Mark 10:21). Self-censoring pastors may be safe from critique, but their reticence leaves God's people to struggle quietly in high-stakes situations without even considering pastoral wisdom. This is too high a price for the Church to pay in its quest for comfort. The new religious marketplace can do better.

When the Church marks important occasions, believers traditionally adjust their day-to-day practices temporarily to show particular reverence through voluntary restraint. Christians across the centuries fasted, for instance, on somber holy days or when the need to make big decisions called for a humble disposition to clear a path for higher wisdom. But the pursuit of comfort in the Church has tamped down this higher impulse.

Churchgoers increasingly see no reason for the practice of faith to be less convenient on certain days than others. Responding to churchgoers' demand for consistent convenience, the Church has lost some of its most important character-building sacrifices. This can be seen in the changing rituals surrounding Lent and funerals.

The season of Lent, the period leading up to Easter, serves as a rehearsal for the self-denying Christian life. The forty-day term is long by design—as long as Jesus' trial in the wilderness with the Devil. The experience isn't supposed to be fun. Themes center on repentance and humility, beginning on Ash Wednesday with the words "remember that you are dust, and to dust you shall return." Since ancient times, Christians have marked the season with acts of self-denial. Fasting, prayer, and almsgiving—all hallmarks of Lent—create opportunities to ponder one's need for a Savior, to practice generosity, and to cultivate gratitude. Individuals and communities have traditionally given up personal pleasures. For example, Catholics fast on Ash Wednesday and Good Friday; Orthodox Christians follow a strict dietary regimen throughout the season. Though some Protestant groups downplay Lent as something Catholics and Orthodox do, many others recognize the season's importance and observe it to one degree or another.

In recent years, Protestants in America have reinvented Lent as a season no more sacrificial than any other. The United Methodist Church and United Church of Christ have developed liturgies for a new day on the calendar: "Passion Sunday."

This frees up churchgoers' schedules by compressing the messages of Palm Sunday, Maundy Thursday, and Good Friday into a single service. But in the process, it reduces to just a few convenient minutes the time set aside in the Christian calendar to remember the Savior's last days. It removes the impetus for Christians to set aside one night a year to ponder what happened at the Last Supper and a second night or lunch hour to remember the Crucifixion. When the faithful take time to worship on these days, they remember together the sacrifice that Jesus willfully incurred for the salvation of the world. But Christians easily miss, on emotional as well as intellectual levels, this connection between Christ's sacrifice and human salvation when they opt for convenience and spend these holy nights as if they were nothing special. They become less cognizant that the One they worship paid an ultimate price and calls them to follow in His Way. This trend toward celebrating Passion Sundays surely satisfies a demand for convenience. But it also contributes to a false understanding of the Gospel: Christians infer from the way holy days are managed that following Christ has no lifestyle implications.

Lenten piety has become yet another opportunity for fun without sacrifice. One Connecticut church, for instance, marked Lent a few years ago by holding an auction to raise $7,000 for a youth-group trip. Church leaders say their congregations increasingly like to receive ashes on their foreheads on Ash Wednesday, but afterward they don't deny themselves even as much as chocolate, a cliché token sacrifice of Lent in decades past. If churchgoers change behavior at all for Lent, pastors have told me, they generally add a self-improvement practice such as getting to the gym more often.

"I don't know anyone who has given anything up for Lent," said Kevan Hitch, former pastor of First & Summerfield United Methodist Church in New Haven, Connecticut. "It's kind of a big joke."

Taking the sacrifice out of Lent destroys a once-a-year opportunity to build humility and stamina. American culture promotes happy, clappy celebrations throughout the year. There is no structured time for introspection or asking whether our boundless self-esteem is really warranted. Lent offers a rare period to reckon with personal and societal sinfulness and to dwell in remorse long enough to thirst for grace. Reinvent this season as one more occasion to celebrate and the Church year no longer contains time to ponder why humankind needs a Savior. Humility and gratitude languish when they are not intentionally cultivated.

Making Lent look like the rest of the year might satisfy demand from the religious marketplace, but over time churchgoers will forget how to use this season to reinforce core values. In a world where pride and greed have led to a financial system's collapse and other devastating consequences, the Church needs to ask whether refashioning religion as a perennial source of comfort is a good idea.

Memorial services don't occur with the same predictable timing as Lent, but they're equally important for affirming Christian values and strengthening spiritual resolve. When survivors gather to bid goodbye to the deceased, the practices they follow testify to their highest ideals as human beings. But attempts to minimize the harder parts of faith have changed even how Christians bury their dead. In the market-driven Church, funereal practices increasingly reflect comfort as a priority over any other value.

Traditional practices at Christian memorials demonstrate confidence in a God more powerful than nature and death. This conviction is most clearly displayed when mourners, in no mood to sing, nevertheless lift their voices in songs of praise. Christian hymns at funerals are symbolic of the Spirit's ability to overcome death, breathing eternal life into believers. The Spirit empowers them to rise above natural instincts such as despair. By rising to sing, Christians give physical expression to their capacity, aided by grace, to do even what is most difficult. In that act, they demonstrate that they are grateful to God no matter how bad circumstances may become. Singing in the midst of grief is both a demonstration of bravery and a rehearsal for braver acts to come.

This tradition of transcending natural impulses at memorial services, like many other traditions, is caving under market pressure. Many a funeral director has told me he has no use for an organ because nobody wants to sing at funerals anymore. Of course, mourners probably never *wanted* to sing, but they did so because they subscribed to a spiritual tradition that understood the act's symbolic power. In recent years the mood of the

bereaved has come to trump theological concerns. This is true
even when memorials happen inside church buildings. Organists often don't need to show up for memorials, as they did a
half century ago. If they play anything, they stick to preludes,
postludes, and anthems to accompany soloists—none of which
require congregational participation, let alone rehearsals of
bravery. This marks a concession to the customers, in this case
the surviving family members. They are sometimes presented
with the option of including singing in the service, but they decide against it because they fear that it would make guests uncomfortable. Few pastors have resisted this trend, perhaps
because it means less work for them as well as organists and
funeral directors. From the new, user-friendly funerals, memorial attendees may easily infer that the Christian life is ultimately all about being comfortable and providing comfort,
since that's what the faithful do when they confront mortality
together. Such inferences would be dead wrong, but they follow
logically from the values put forward in a customer-sensitive
marketplace.

With help from market forces, modern memorials have
come to sacralize the wishes of the deceased. This isn't just a
matter of keeping Uncle Phil's casket closed because that's
what he said he wanted. Families routinely expect these worship services to reflect a loved one's preferences in everything
from flowers to theology (e.g., minimal references to God when
the deceased wasn't a believer). The results can be jarring. At
one memorial service I officiated, the brother-in-law of the

deceased delivered the eulogy and pretended to channel the dead man. "'When are we gonna quit all this bullshit and get something to eat?' That's what he would be saying right now," the eulogist explained as I silently winced. It went on like that for a painful forty minutes. The gathered crowd heard nothing of the Gospel or of God's promises, which would have been a source of strength for the days ahead, especially since this particular death had been a shocking suicide. Other speakers maintained the same crass informality in an effort to make the ceremony more comfortable, but the result was an occasion deprived of its power to heal and strengthen. This case reflected remarkably bad judgment, but it nevertheless illustrates a widespread problem. Communities don't hear the highest values reaffirmed at memorials when they let the fears and idiosyncrasies of one individual be their sole guide for the occasion. The market-driven Church ends up squandering opportunities to teach core values against the sobering backdrop of death.

Even when it comes to burial, increasing demand for inexpensive cremations has led to a decrease in rituals that testify to transcendent hope and costly discipleship. Christians have since ancient times buried their dead whenever possible with bodies intact and facing east. This reflects the understanding that Christ is prophesied to return from the east and raise the faithful on Judgment Day. Each time this custom is repeated, believers proclaim confidence in the spiritual tradition that inspired it. It may not always be convenient or cost-efficient to bury the dead in this manner, yet when Christians make sacrifices to do so anyway, they bear witness to a Way that isn't always easy.

Pragmatic concerns increasingly prevail in today's marketplace. Cremation rates are rising fastest, by as much as 25 percent annually, in states with high percentages of Protestants, such as Mississippi, Alabama, and Tennessee. In 2006, 34 percent of dead bodies in the United States and Canada were cremated; the Cremation Association of North America expects that number to rise to 59 percent by 2025.

Sometimes, of course, practical considerations must reign supreme, such as when a family can't afford a traditional burial. Nonetheless, the marketplace's apparent disregard for burial of the intact body as an important Christian ritual is troubling. People making decisions about burial services probably aren't aware that anything theological is at stake. Unlike fifty years ago, when clergy offered guidance in such matters, today survivors bear sole responsibility—whether they know it or not—for determining the role of the Church in American cemeteries. Not surprisingly, that role is fading along with so many other elements of Church life that no longer compel meaningful sacrifice.

Comfort has become a central goal of worship. In the face of life's challenges, people come to church seeking therapy or comforting affirmation. They often get their wish because church leaders know that these customers will vanish from the padded seats if they're not satisfied.

An episode at a Minnesota megachurch illustrates how demand for comforting sermons can hinder the Church's ability to bear witness and save souls. Woodland Hills Church is a Southern Baptist congregation in the Twin Cities area. In the run-up to the 2004 election, Woodland Hills' Pastor Gregory Boyd refused to toe a socially conservative line in his congregation, which at the time attracted about 5,000 weekly attendees. He preached a six-part sermon on the importance of keeping religion out of culture wars and politics.

Parishioners were outraged that he wouldn't champion their anti-abortion and anti-gay marriage causes, according to a July 2006 *New York Times* report. They wanted the comforting experience of hearing their political views echoed and sanctioned from the pulpit. Disappointed, they fled. About 20 percent quit the church altogether. They stopped giving, too: a $7 million capital campaign fell $3 million short of its goal. Strapped for cash, the church laid off 14 percent of its fifty-person staff. Twenty volunteers, including key Sunday-school teachers, stopped serving in protest of Reverend Boyd's apolitical message. When faced with a challenge to grow by considering a new approach to faithfulness, churchgoers rejected the opportunity and brought down a variety of ministries in the process.

This widely reported case offered a cautionary tale for church leaders. The apparent lesson: don't try to expand your people's concepts of faithfulness. In the end, all that is to be gained by challenging people is heartache and stress. Perhaps

it's better—at least if your goal is a stable career in ministry—
to emulate the thousands of leaders who don't make it into the
New York Times because they're comforting their people as re-
quested. Such an approach would suit today's culture. Americans of all political stripes flock not only to news sources that
reflect their views, but also to ideological enclaves where they
are surrounded by like-minded people who supply steady affirmation. If being affirmed is that important to parishioners,
then pastors will presumably do well to provide affirmation
from the pulpit. Of course, such an unholy agreement between
preachers and their flocks betrays the Gospel's challenging
essence, but it's easy to see how both sides have been tempted
in light of Woodland Hills' ordeal.

Some may argue that preachers aren't always so quick to
offer comfort without challenging their congregation. They'll
point to the many sermons that discuss sin as evidence of an
enduring willingness to address difficult and challenging topics.
Evangelicals, for instance, preach on the sin of practicing homosexuality. In contrast, Unitarians denounce the sin of homo-
phobia, along with the sins of racism and sexism. These
preachers run the risk of offending people in their congregations, yet they forge ahead. This, some would say, proves that a
culture of seeking comfort in the Church hasn't rendered sermons unchallenging.

Yet this argument overlooks the self-selecting nature of
these congregations. Sermons denouncing homosexuality are
comforting to many conservative, heterosexual couples, just as

sermons proclaiming that God blesses gay relationships are comforting to liberals with gay friends. People reasonably leave church feeling like the self-righteous Pharisee who prayed, "'God, I thank you that I am not like other people: swindlers, unjust, adulterers, or even like this tax collector" (Luke 18:9-14).

Even when a pastor aims to challenge the gathered flock, audiences derive comfort by assuming that the challenging message doesn't apply to them. Church consultant Tom Bandy found that pastors across North America were raising themes of humility and greed during the Great Recession of 2008–09, and were routinely frustrated by their lack of impact. "Pastors are saying that when they speak about greed or consumers, everyone in the congregation points to the other guy," Bandy told me at the time. "It's really tough to bring it home." The widespread eagerness to receive comfort from the Church is preventing exhortation from getting through to those who need it.

After a comforting sermon, churchgoers often receive the Sacrament of Communion, also known as the Lord's Supper. Traditionally, to be eligible to receive Communion, a churchgoer was expected to adhere to a high standard of moral behavior; this inspired the faithful to embrace the difficulties of living out their faith. The Sacrament now serves a more therapeutic purpose as high behavioral standards get pushed aside.

Biblical instructions for the Lord's Supper emphasize the need for partakers of Communion to prepare by cultivating virtue. The Apostle Paul chastises the Corinthians for harboring "divisions among you" even as they partake of the sacred meal. Such rifts harm the integrity of the Church, which should be one spiritual body of believers. He admonishes each person present to examine him- or herself *before* receiving Communion, "for he who eats and drinks in an unworthy manner eats and drinks judgment to himself, not discerning the Lord's body" (1 Corinthians 11:29). In practice, Christians living up to their callings through the ages would go to one another and settle their individual differences—through confession, forgiveness, and/or making amends—in order to receive the Sacrament in a worthy manner. Such actions require humility and grace. Thus, the desire to receive Sacrament compels believers to cultivate virtue and expand their hearts. It edifies, not by magic, but by summoning Christ's followers to a costly, higher way of managing all relationships.

The consumer-driven Church jettisons these character-shaping dynamics when it refashions the Sacrament as an easy source of comfort. When I arrived at Union Church as pastor in September 2000, there were no standards of conduct for Communion takers. On Communion Sundays, anyone who happened to be in the building—regardless of age, beliefs, commitments, or simmering conflicts—was welcome to partake. This policy was supposed to reflect God's unconditional love. The symbolic meal was open to all and cost nothing. The unintended but implicit message was that grace is cheap.

Prior to my arrival, deacons used to bring the bread and wine to the Sunday school, where kids swarmed and grabbed as if the holy elements were cookies and Kool-Aid. After worship, a deacon would sometimes feed consecrated bread to garbage-picking gulls. No one intended disrespect; these practices were supposed to show God's lavish, unconditional love for all creatures. Yet the idea of the Sacrament as something special enough to inspire self-restraint or even special handling was long gone. One of the Church's most important tools for shaping Christian character had lost its edge and become, for all practical purposes, a cheap form of comfort.

When I tried to raise the standards for Communion, I realized that the existing policy was a reflection of the congregation's demands. Deacons, perhaps grudgingly, supported my initiative to begin "fencing the Table"—that is, serving the Lord's Supper only to those of decision making age (thirteen or older) who had decided to be followers of Christ. The goal was to reconnect the Sacrament with the behaviors of discipleship, such as making peace regularly with one's adversaries. But our efforts bore little fruit.

Immediately, members protested that children were losing a ritual they enjoyed. Some grumbled that unbaptized adults, who had enjoyed the congregation's "anything goes" style, wouldn't feel welcome anymore. I responded that these individuals should get baptized since the Church is, after all, about making disciples, but my case fell on deaf ears. Parishioners demanded a Communion policy that would indicate only that God loves them regardless of their beliefs or actions. As the one who tried to raise the bar, I faced resentment for as long as I was at the church.

Mainline denominations have lowered Communion standards in response to marketplace pressures. The United Methodist Church, for instance, no longer restricts the Sacrament to the baptized. UMC congregations now offer it to any worshipper who professes to have faith in Christ, without regard to age. Such shifts in policy tend to mirror shifts in attendance. As a denomination shrinks, it lowers Communion standards in order to be more welcoming, only to lose even more members. For example, the Evangelical Lutheran Church in America has for more than forty years been steadily losing members. Simultaneously, it has been welcoming more people to its Communion table. In 1970, only adolescents and adults who had confirmed their baptism could receive the Lord's Supper in ELCA congregations. Today, even baptized infants may partake with parental consent, and parents appreciate the inclusiveness of this option.

Presbyterians have also eliminated behavioral expectations related to the Sacrament. In the nineteenth century, admission to the Presbyterian Communion table required a physical token, which one received from an elder who could vouch for the partaker's ongoing efforts to be repentant and forgiving. Now the Sacrament is offered to members of the Presbyterian Church (U.S.A.) with no such expectations: all of the baptized are welcome.

Though I've attended dozens of Communion services in various denominations in the past decade, I've never heard a pastor remind the faithful that those who haven't resolved personal conflicts should abstain. Across the board, the Church has anxiously backed away from expectations that once encouraged virtuous habits among partakers. As a result, to partake is to feel welcome, but not welcomed into a robust community that is walking together in a common, costly Way. That community no longer exists.

Comfort will always have a place in the Church. In times of tragedy, the Church rightly soothes Christians with assurances from their ever-faithful God. The challenge, going forward, will be to preserve that dynamic while reinstituting discipline that's not always comfortable.

To achieve this balance, the Church may need only to draw on what churchgoers already know from Scripture and from experience. They know from Paul's letter to the Romans that "suffering produces perseverance; perseverance produces character; character produces hope. And hope does not disappoint" (Romans 5:3–5). They know from experience, in settings from school to the playing field to the office, that the most comfortable path isn't always the right one or the most beneficial one. These insights may come to mind more readily in churchgoers' roles as coworkers or managers than in their roles as consumers, since shoppers seldom look for a costly path. But there may be room in the psyches of religious consumers to recognize a need for the Church to be more than a comforting influence.

It will take time to reform the contemporary Church. The Church, perhaps more than any other institution, carries immense historical baggage. From the Crusades to the Inquisition, it's been an agent of great discomfort. Present-day parishioners who blame Church teachings or practices for their personal pain may vehemently resist efforts to make the Church into something other than a benign source of comfort. But there is an urgent need to do just that, since no other institution—not government, not media, not schools—will pick up the slack and proactively shape people's characters. The Church must overcome both its baggage and its present tendency to pander in order to become a character-shaping force in the twenty-first century. Perhaps stakeholders will use the marketplace to make that happen after considering the harm unfolding under the status quo.

CHAPTER 4

A Bumper Crop of Weak Moral Character

EARLY IN MAY 2009, FIVE LEADERS FROM THE NATIONAL Religious Campaign Against Torture hastily convened a press conference. A new survey from the Pew Research Center had illuminated a stunning reality: 71 percent of Americans said torture of suspected terrorists could be justified. And among those willing to support the use of torture, Christians were at the head of the pack.

The data suggested that the vast majority of American Christians condone torturing suspects. A full 79 percent of white evangelicals deemed torture to be acceptable in certain cases. Mainline Christians, despite the left-leaning politics of their denominational leaders, gave their blessing as well: 63 percent approved of the use of torture. The data also showed a strong connection between active churchgoing and support for torture. Respondents who said they attended religious services—whether weekly, monthly, or even just a few times a year—were more likely to approve of torture than those who said they seldom if ever attend. In other words, the more one goes to church, the more likely one is to support torture.

"The resources of the Christian faith have not been adequately mobilized by the leaders of our churches," said David P. Gushee, an evangelical ethicist at Mercer University and member of the anti-torture campaign. "We need a deepened commitment to prayer for our churches. We need to address the moral formation of our people and our clergy ... and [we need a] deepening of the moral and spiritual vision of dignity and sacredness in every human life, especially those lives that we're tempted to consider unworthy of such dignity."

Christian leaders across the theological spectrum recognized that something had gone terribly wrong. How could it be that followers of the Prince of Peace sanction cruelty in the name of justice? They were troubled to think that their Christian brothers and sisters might harbor more tolerance for torture than members of other faiths and people of no faith. Left-leaning religious leaders at the press conference worried aloud that their followers might have been disproportionately influenced by conservative talk radio. Prominent voices on the religious right, such as the Southern Baptists' top ethicist, Richard Land, tried to awaken consciences by denouncing torture as morally wrong under all circumstances. But neither side had much to say about why the Church, for all its fundraising prowess and importance in Americans' lives, has become so ineffective at shaping noble values within its own immediate sphere of influence.

Based on raw numbers and signs of popularity, the Church should be having a profound impact on its people's concerns and priorities. Megachurches, with their upbeat worship services and small groups tailored to personal preferences, have figured out a winning formula for growth. Only 310 megachurches existed in 1990. By 2007, the count had reached 1,250. Megachurches provide a spiritual home for some 4.5 million weekly attendees, including many newcomers to Christianity. Across the board, Americans attend church in greater numbers than their counterparts in other Western nations. Such data depict America as a religious nation where the Church is important to people and presumably influences how they live.

In several cases, the Church is growing on the denominational level, too. Denominations as varied as the Pentecostal Assemblies of God, the conservative Southern Baptist Convention, and the liberal Unitarian Universalist Association (which includes some Christians) all report increases in membership in recent years. These patterns contrast sharply with those of liberal mainline Protestantism, which has been watching membership rolls contract since the 1960s. But growth among a diverse handful of denominations nevertheless underscores the fact that independent, quasi-entrepreneurial congregations aren't the only ones penetrating new markets these days. For organizations with a resonant message, opportunities seem ripe for having a powerful impact.

In politics, the Church has seemingly become a formidable force on the right and left alike. Successful campaigns to block gay marriage and to raise the federal minimum wage testify in part to the power of churches in legislative arenas. Troubled observers worry that the Church has built up *too much* influence in American society and even poses a threat to the founders' intentions to keep church and state separate. They fear that religious encroachment in areas from scientific research to public education is instilling faith-based values where they don't belong.

But a closer look reveals just how nominal the Church's influence in the lives of its people has become. When the Church is true to its mission, it elicits the gifts of the Holy Spirit: love, joy, peace, patience, kindness, goodness, faithfulness, gentleness, and self-control (Galatians 5:22). Yet this widespread support for torture suggests that patience, self-control, and other holy traits are disturbingly rare in the Church of the twenty-first century. A strong correlation has emerged between the consumer-driven religious marketplace and the decay of Christian moral character. This becomes clear when one looks to see whether traditional virtues still mark the lives of those who practice the faith.

For many virtuous traits, self-control serves as a foundation. From it comes much of what everyone hopes to see in a Christian: fortitude to resist temptation, for example, or to love when others succumb to hate. Without it, surmounting the challenges of discipleship would be impossible. But in the new religious marketplace, churches are failing to teach Christians to act with self-control in even the most basic areas of life.

An epidemic of overeating among Christians highlights a basic lack of self-control. Obesity has become rampant among American Protestants. Nearly one in five Methodists is obese, according to a 2006 Purdue University study. Among Baptists, it's more than one in four. Meanwhile, fewer than one in 100 American Hindus, Jews, Muslims, and Buddhists are obese. Even when allowing for geographical considerations, the research found Protestants to be fatter than people of other religious backgrounds.

The clergy have set a bad example—about 75 percent of clerics in America are either overweight or obese. This is not a minor problem, as pastors' poor eating habits are raising churches' costs and detracting from ministry efforts. The Evangelical Lutheran Church in America, the country's third-largest Protestant denomination, has warned that overweight and otherwise unhealthy clergy are threatening the church's future as costs associated with clergy health care encroach on mission-outreach budgets.

The Church needs to acknowledge its failure to help Christians fight food-related temptation. Even though obesity is no more common in the Church than in American society at large, the Church has a duty to help its people rise above their animalistic impulses. In church, Christians should be learning that the root of dignity is the ability to say no to oneself. Instead, churches notoriously entice their people to gorge themselves at potluck dinners, where processed foods abound, and to graze on piles of doughnuts after worship on Sundays. Disregarded is the long Christian tradition of fasting as a means of building one's willpower for future challenges. Serving up deliciously fattening food satisfies a clientele that likes fried foods and sweets, but it neglects that clientele's spiritual formation. As a result, Christians learn habits of primal weakness in the very environment that is supposed to strengthen them against their lower natures.

Money mismanagement, another sign of weak or undeveloped self-control, is also rife in Christian households. Even before the financial crisis of 2008, Christians were already swimming in debt and looking to financial rescue services for help. At Christian Credit Counselors, Inc., in Southfield, Michigan, the average customer is an "overextended" thirtysomething woman who owes $25,000 to $35,000 on credit cards. Crown Financial Ministries serves more than 2 million U.S. Christians and has been growing its client base by about 25 percent per year during this decade. Dozens of organizations have formed over the past fifteen years to serve Christians who face financial disaster as a result of overspending. Apparently churchgoers aren't learning even enough self-control to keep themselves and their families fiscally secure.

Church members' excessive indebtedness once again indicts the Church's weak influence on character. Truly effective churches would have coached Christ's followers to be content with what they can afford (1 Timothy 6). They wouldn't have needed to offer emergency classes in money management to help members manage out-of-control debts, as hundreds of congregations did in 2008 and 2009. To be sure, a fraction of the population has dug deeply into debt for reasons other than weak willpower. But the sheer numbers of debt-swamped Christians suggest many aren't victims of medical disaster or other circumstances beyond their control. More germane is the Church's failure to teach lifestyles of restraint. When the economy was humming and Christians were racking up personal debts, the Church was mostly mum—as if succumbing to temptations to overspend were not a serious spiritual problem. Now the Church is trying to play catch-up after having turned a blind eye when its people were jeopardizing their futures and asking the institution only for affirmation and amusement.

Scriptures have much to say about managing desires for money and the things it can buy. The tenth commandment says one shall not covet his neighbor's house, servants, animals, or other possessions (Exodus 20:17). The Letter to the Hebrews advises: "Keep your lives free from the love of money, and be content with what you have, because God has said, 'Never will I leave you; never will I forsake you.'" (Hebrews 13:5). Paul writes to Timothy: "People who want to get rich fall into temptation and a trap and into many foolish and harmful desires that plunge men into ruin and destruction" (1 Timothy 6:9). But precious few churches have designed small groups to help people discover the joys of needing and wanting less. In the absence of customer demand for this type of education, the Church merely stands by as the spiritual disease of materialism festers among its people.

Young Christians, too, display moral weaknesses that implicate an ineffective Church. High-school students who attend Christian schools (and presumably have grown up attending church) are more likely than their counterparts in secular schools to have cheated on an exam, according to a 2002 survey from the Josephson Institute of Ethics. More than seven out of every ten Christian students in the survey admitted to having cheated in school.

This seems unthinkable in an age when the Church, at least in conservative circles, touts the importance of maintaining personal holiness. But Christian students who cheat are just as willing as non-Christians to prioritize easy rewards ahead of personal sacrifice and hard work. They want success in a world where job candidates routinely lie on résumés, athletes take performance-enhancing drugs, and ministers steal sermons off the Internet. Even though the Church may not be actively teaching young people to cheat, it's also not convincing them of the need to suffer, even modestly, for their principles. The Church's customers still get the mood boost they seek on Sundays, but the lack of demand for tougher messages seems to be taking a toll on the character of a rising generation.

Christian adults are also drifting away from the idea that moral behavior involves personal sacrifice. In matters of money, for instance, today's American Christians are less convinced

than prior generations of Christians that doing right sometimes means doing without. According to the World Values
Survey, in 1980 one of the groups most likely to say it's never
justifiable to accept a bribe, cheat on taxes, claim government
benefits without entitlement, or ride public transportation
without paying was the churchgoing population. But in the
World Values Survey of 2000, any such correlation between
church attendance and financial morality had nearly disappeared. Sociological research links this trend to the Church's
declining influence in the area of personal finance. Congregants grew more concerned about other people's abortions and
euthanasia than about the morality of their own tax-paying
and other financial habits.

Churchgoers also use pornography to a degree that suggests
they see little need for self-denial. According to xxxchurch.com,
a Web-based ministry for porn-addicted Christians, 48 percent
of Christian families say pornography is a major problem in
their homes. One magazine for pastors found in a readership
survey that one in three pastors admit to struggling with
pornography. The problem has grown pervasive enough to warrant a national tour in 2005 by two crusading pastors who
drew huge crowds to churches across the country and to a National Porn Sunday event. Apparently the Church's focus on
pleasing customers isn't enough to prevent them from pleasing
themselves whenever possible.

Even with regard to marriage, a cause célèbre of many
churches in recent years, the behavior of believers doesn't seem

to be shaped by church teachings. Born-again Christians are every bit as likely as members of the general population to get divorced (the divorce rate is about 32 percent), according to a 2007–08 survey of 3,792 adults interviewed by the Barna Group, a Christian research firm. That conclusion reinforced what Barna had found three and thirteen years earlier, as well as in tracking studies during the intervening years. Some academics question Barna's methods and point instead to other data that suggest Christians are somewhat less likely than non-Christians to divorce. But even Barna's critics concede that one in three Christians who attend church weekly get divorced. The indisputable fact is that Christians divorce at a rate that is antithetical to their tradition's teachings. That unfortunate reality strikes a sensitive chord, especially for evangelicals, who as recently as fifty years ago preached that divorce was a terrible sin to be resisted. They've since mostly purged that rhetoric as their pews have filled with divorced people whom preachers can't afford to offend. As Barna Group founder George Barna rightly acknowledges in his analysis, the Church is not effectively shaping the hearts of people who choose married life.

These findings about obesity, personal finance, youth cheating, pornography, and divorce point only to areas of Christian life where researchers have gathered and analyzed recent data. Much more could be said about how churchgoers' consumptive lifestyles and self-centered habits barely differ from those of their non-Christian neighbors. I wish I could say Christians exhibit greater virtue in their public lives than in their private ones. But unfortunately, the corrosive effects of a religious marketplace characterized by bargain hunting don't end with personal morality.

Christians are meant to be peacemakers, according to the Gospel. Jesus' prayer for the disciples asks, "That they may all be one ... so that the world may believe that you have sent me" (John 17:21). He teaches followers how to work out their differences (Matthew 18). He chastises them when they fight one another for positions of power (Mark 9). Across history, Christians have understood Him as the world's Reconciler, and some who've insisted on peacemaking in His name have eventually earned respect in due proportion. St. Francis is widely revered today for having found a harmony that transcends boundaries of class and even species. Pacifists, such as the Mennonites and the Amish, remain controversial, but their lack of persecution in modern times testifies to the respect they've earned through adherence to principle. Ecumenists of the twentieth century, such as the Council on Christian Unity's former president Paul A. Crow, enjoyed reputations as people who understood the heart of their Savior and therefore worked tirelessly for unity among His followers.

Peaceful ideals notwithstanding, conflict among Christians has become institutionalized in new ways over the past quarter century. Fierce denominational infighting has gone from being an occasional disturbance to a staple of annual meetings as sexuality and other hot-button issues forever rankle entrenched opponents.

Acrimony festers on the congregational level, too. In the United Church of Christ, ministers who oversee more than a dozen congregations have told me they spend more and more time—50 to 75 percent of their working hours—dealing with congregational infighting. Such an embittered state of affairs has become the norm in a range of Protestant settings. In a 2006 survey of Protestants who had quit attending a particular congregation, the chief reason cited was that fellow churchgoers were hypocritical and/or judgmental (which easily can be read to mean: I felt hurt and fled conflict). These signs point to a Christian community that's increasingly squeamish about doing the hard work of forgiveness and reconciliation. To an unsettling degree, the Church isn't shaping its people into peacemakers.

To be sure, conflict in the Church is hardly a new development. The Apostle Paul found plenty of it in the congregations he founded, as scriptural letters to the Corinthians attest. Recent snapshots of congregational life in America suggest churches were no more or less conflicted in 2006 than they were in 1998—or in colonial times, for that matter. Some degree of conflict is to be expected in the Church as long as human nature endures.

What's new in today's churches, however, is the growing presence of special-interest organizations with a stake in making sure the conflict never ends. Over the past few decades, to give voice to churchgoers' disparate agendas, dozens of well-funded parachurch organizations have taken root. Their job is to advocate for supporters' causes, and their existence effectively guarantees that conflict will persist among those who champion opposing agendas. The politically conservative Institute on Religion & Democracy, founded in 1982, provides a steady stream of well-funded criticism of mainline denominations for their left-leaning political goals and alliances. On the left, the National Council of Churches is a reliable opponent of the IRD. These two groups have bitterly accused one another of being a front organization for foundations with partisan agendas.

Within denominations, such organizations are just as pervasive. Groups such as Integrity (pro-gay Episcopalians), Presbyterians Pro-Life (anti-abortion), and Lutheran CORE (opposing openly gay clergy) fight endlessly to get their constituents' desires reflected in church policies and practices. In effect, they force churchgoers to take sides, harden their positions on divisive issues, and see fellow believers either as enemies to be defeated or as targets to be won over. Expanding hearts, admitting mistakes, and seeking forgiveness all become increasingly unlikely in such charged environments. Yet religious consumers have—perhaps unwittingly or unknowingly in some cases—established structures and reinforced patterns that blunt the Church's core mission in pursuit of other causes.

Not all conflict is political. A more subtle manifestation of interdenominational conflict is the strident competition for fickle customers. Branding has become a focal project for denominations as they seek to differentiate themselves. This sometimes means inviting tension by communicating how and why one church body is more appealing than another. During the Catholic clergy's sexual-abuse crisis in 2004, the United Church of Christ rolled out a not-so-subtle advertisement apparently targeting disillusioned Catholics. The ad depicted a church, suggestively Catholic in its Gothic-style architecture, where a bouncer turns away gays, racial minorities, and disabled persons at the entry. It was misleading. The Catholic Church is a leader in racial diversity, while the UCC is more than 90 percent white. And the Catholic Church doesn't turn away gays or the disabled. Such a pejorative ad campaign betrayed the UCC principle of ecumenism—expressed in the motto "that they may all be one"—by seeking to exploit one of Catholicism's darkest hours.

In the new religious marketplace, the UCC—which has steadily been losing members for forty-five years—depends for its survival on an inflow of disgruntled Catholics. This example highlights how competition for customers, who are increasingly willing to switch denominations, creates a steady pressure to undercut others' ministries. When the Church capitulates to such pressure, it models for its people bridge-burning instead of bridge-building, and individual moral character gets none of the strengthening it needs.

Even on an interpersonal level, habits gleaned from the religious marketplace make church conflicts increasingly tough to resolve. Two teachers in my congregation's Sunday school who were close friends had a big falling-out. News travels fast in a small church, and everyone promptly wanted to see the rift patched up. The situation presented a real-life opportunity for these teachers to model what they'd been teaching: humility, forgiveness, ever-expanding love for neighbor. But both opted instead to avoid the situation and seek spiritual sustenance elsewhere. One quit the church immediately; the other withdrew from active church life for more than a year. Each blamed the other and took no personal risks to attempt reconciliation. Running away from the problem was irresistibly easy.

Fleeing conflict in this manner, and therefore failing to deal with it, wasn't uncommon in my congregation. Families and individuals would sometimes disappear for months at a time when they didn't get their way on one issue or another. Such habits seemed traceable to a sentiment I heard spoken aloud often at Union: "This is *our* church." The implication was that churchgoers had a right to get their way and to quit when they were disappointed. Greater appreciation for the Church as God's, not ours, might have helped these churchgoers endure necessary tension at times. But a consumerist sensibility seemed to block their capacities to work through conflict and make peace, as Christianity should be teaching them to do.

Christian life involves not only resolving conflict but also breaking down social barriers as a witness to the radical equality that the Savior has established across humankind. Since its earliest days, the Church has striven to reflect the scriptural principle that "there is no longer Jew or Greek, there is no longer slave or free, there is no longer male or female; for all of you are one in Christ Jesus" (Galatians 3:28). So powerful was this understanding for the early church that congregations accorded Gentiles equal status with members of Jewish backgrounds—a radical idea for the time. As further witness, Paul encouraged early Christians to deal fairly even with slaves, a concept far ahead of his time (Colossians 4:1). Because God had conquered death, the ultimate chasm, those strengthened by His Spirit would bear witness by dismantling division on Earth in visible ways.

Testimony to this principle is waning in the twenty-first-century Church as its customers demand environments filled with people like themselves. A representative example comes from Forest Hill Church, an evangelical congregation in Charlotte, North Carolina. When young adults indicated a preference for worshipping separately from people their parents' ages and older, Forest Hill designed a new congregation just for them. They located it in a converted trucking terminal and gave it a hip name: Warehouse 242. Now Christians in their twenties and thirties can sip coffee during worship, ponder art on a projection screen, and listen to sermons that include tracks from U2 and clips from familiar films. These young believers are apparently getting much of what they want from church: a cool environment unencumbered by stodgy authority figures. But they're paying a high price for their designer religious experience.

By walling themselves off from older members of the community during worship, they're losing a wealth of valuable experience. They're not grappling with the Gospel's social implications by worshipping, for example, alongside blacks and whites who came of age in Charlotte in the days of Jim Crow. They're not hearing the Gospel's emotional power refracted through someone else's music, which could help connect them with truths that transcend fleeting cultural touchstones. Their immediate wants are being indulged, but not reformed to reflect God's own. Surely they're getting what they want as consumers, but they're impoverishing themselves and the Church in the process.

Niche churches such as Warehouse 242 are proliferating and catering to ever-narrower market segments. Devotees of cowboy culture, for instance, can find like-minded people at the 145 churches that have started meeting in barns or riding arenas and baptizing people in horse troughs since the first one, Cowboy Church of Ellis County (Texas), was organized in March 2000. Bikers in Irving, Texas, don't have to worry about mixing with prim church ladies, since Hope Fellowship Church exists to serve Christian motorcyclists. Those who attend megachurches might see diversity around them at worship, but when it's time to actually get to know each other, that often happens in highly tailored affinity groups. Whether a person is into golf, parenting, or networking with fellow lawyers, he or she will soon be rubbing elbows exclusively with those who share his or her interests and/or background.

Narrowly defined church communities may make people comfortable in the short term, but they do nothing to expand a person's capacity to love someone quite different from him- or herself. A person can go through the entire megachurch or niche-church experience and never once have to cross a cultural barrier. Jesus counseled wariness of this trap. He taught that there's nothing special about loving one's friends and family: even tax collectors and pagans do that (Matthew 5:46-47). It is more godly to love the unlovable—or at least to learn to do so by taking incremental steps. But the market-driven Church has created a cultural architecture that makes such progress highly unlikely, if not impossible.

Despite mountains of evidence that suggests the Church is thwarting its own mission by bowing to misguided consumer pressure, churches keep striving to please—rather than lead— their clientele. Between 1996 and 2006, more than 20,000 congregations hired consultants from Outreach, Inc., in Vista, California, to bring corporate-style marketing, such as direct mail, to their outreach campaigns. The most highly recruited church leaders are often those with marketing backgrounds and proven track records for promoting organizations via new and traditional media. One pastor, for instance, told me he was offered a plum ministry position in Maryland after he touted his success with outdoor advertising in Amarillo, Texas, and Las Vegas.

Gimmicks and giveaways represent churches as organizations offering pleasurable experiences and asking almost nothing in return. The New Life Christian Church in Centreville, Virginia, spent $10,000 on an ice-cream truck and painted the church's name on it. They then gave away free ice cream in order to "make God's love real." In Charlotte, North Carolina, LifePointe Christian Church once gave away 3,000 water bottles and 5,000 Frisbees emblazoned with the church's logo and contact information. Such corporate-style public-relations efforts aim to present the Church as a purveyor of great treats and fun. While that's sure to grab attention, it betrays the Church's mission, which is to train people to love as God loves through processes that often aren't fun. Giveaways may bring in a few warm bodies, but they also set the stage for customers to demand more cheap fun or leave disappointed. Either way, the Church suffers.

On the denominational level, churches have been marketing themselves as anything but challenging. Denominations have rolled out big-budget television campaigns in recent years to build their name recognition and attract new members. Their messages try to blunt the reputation of churches as judgmental places and position them instead as bastions of unconditional love. The United Methodist Church claims to consist of "Open Minds, Open Hearts, Open Doors." The Unitarian Universalist Association tagline is "Nurture Your Spirit. Help Heal Our World." The United Church of Christ insists: "No matter who you are, or where you are on life's journey, you're welcome here." All these messages evoke feelings of cozy comfort; churches are suggesting they'll be challenge-free zones. Churches affiliated with these denominations are sure to have a hard time elevating hearts when newcomers, having seen ads produced on Madison Avenue, arrive expecting an easy path.

Church leaders insist that mass marketing is necessary in this age of fierce competition for busy people's attention. "Evangelicals are marketers because they're really passionate about their product," said H. B. London, vice president of ministry outreach and pastoral ministries at Focus on the Family, when I interviewed him in 2005. "The Church in more ways than not is mirroring Wall Street and the world and Madison Avenue" to get its message out

The hope is that effective marketing can get people in the door, and satisfying experiences inside can keep them coming back. But this approach leaves no room for the Church to fulfill its true purpose of shaping hearts. By promising people affirmation and more of what they already want, the Church takes itself out of the business of challenging Christ's followers on the level of the will. Newcomers will feel betrayed if they're told, after having responded to sweet enticements, that the life of faith is actually a sacrificial one. Hence, churches with slick marketing appeals often box themselves into a position of powerlessness on the level that really matters.

Marketing might benefit individual congregations in terms of numeric growth, but the trend correlates more broadly with an exodus from church life in America. The ranks of self-identifying Christians have shrunk dramatically in recent years. In 1990, 86 percent of all Americans identified themselves as

Christians; by 2008, that number had declined to 76 percent, according to the American Religious Identification Survey 2008. A full 90 percent of those who quit the faith in that period were non-Catholics—i.e., mostly Protestants.

The survey data points to tough times for the very organizations that have lowered expectations in attempts to be more welcoming. Mainline Protestants, for instance, lost a quarter of their market share in just seven years, dropping from 17.2 percent of the U.S. population in 2001 to just 12.9 percent in 2008. While some people may be switching churches, others seem to be getting disillusioned and dropping out of organized religion altogether. The percentage of Americans claiming no religion has almost doubled from 8 in 1990 to 15 in 2008. Other research, based on Sunday-morning head counts rather than surveys, concludes that church attendance is lower than polls suggest and is dropping. In 1990, about 20 percent of Americans were in church on any given Sunday, according to the American Church Research Project. By 2005, the percentage of Americans attending church weekly was down to 17.5. The ACRP forecast, which sees population growing faster than America's congregations, expects just 10 percent of Americans to be in church on an average Sunday in 2050. The broad trend of removing sacrifice from Christianity may be pleasing certain market niches in the short run, but the long-term outlook for a faith made ultra-easy is bleak.

Churches continue to measure success by attendance and revenue figures, even though such obsessions with numbers have done much to marginalize the Church's influence on souls. Just as *Inc.* magazine annually ranks the fastest-growing technology companies, *Outreach* magazine ranks America's fastest-growing congregations in a special issue. Churches on this list gain fame by growing rapidly, as Granger Community Church in South Bend, Indiana, has. Average attendance at Granger swelled from 2,000 in 2000 to 5,700 in 2006. "At Granger, we've decided we'll be more effective if we try to learn a new language [of hip culture], and it seems to be working," said Tony Morgan, former pastor of administrative services. Granger's formula involves staples of the customer-driven church, such as small groups that emphasize fun conversation and no commitment beyond a single session. Granger, like other fast-growing churches, has become an object of fascination for church leaders who figure they'd better learn from the likes of Granger or prepare to go extinct.

"Without satisfied customers," reads one church-marketing manual, "the organizations will soon find themselves customer-less and tailspin into oblivion."

To stay competitive, legions of preachers keep marketing manuals near their Bibles. Executive pastors of the nation's fastest-growing churches consistently cite Seth Godin's book, *Purple Cow: Transform Your Business by Being Remarkable*, as one of their most formative influences. Some also read such texts as *Applebee's America: How Successful Political, Business, and Religious Leaders Connect with the New American Community*, which implies that the Church is just another enterprise trying to make a sale.

"Whether your product is a candidate, a hamburger, or the word of God, the challenge is the same," write *Applebee's* authors Douglas B. Sosnik, Matthew J. Dowd, and Ron Fournier. "How do you connect with a fast-changing public and get them to buy what you're selling?"

In this landscape, how can the Church once again compel individuals to embrace the challenging ways of discipleship? Churches of all stripes insist that they already do challenge members, but evidence of their negligible impact makes those arguments ring hollow. Religious consumers need new influences to lead them beyond comfort and help them become better people.

Some argue that the Church is already compelling meaningful sacrifice in successful "high-cost" churches. These include Seventh-day Adventist congregations and many fundamentalist communities whose strict behavioral codes set their people apart from most of secular society. Scholarly research finds that this strictness enhances participation in church life, weeds out "free riders" who scarcely support the ministry, and succeeds in instilling robust moral values. Conversely, the same research shows that communities with lax standards have virtually no impact on their members' moral values. Others say it's a myth that megachurches "water down the faith." Megachurch participants are indeed more likely than other churchgoers to tithe and adhere to private devotional disciplines. These indicators may suggest that the new religious marketplace is attracting more than comfort-seeking churchgoers.

Critics of my argument might claim that the success of high-cost churches proves that hearts are indeed being shaped, sometimes profoundly, within or even because of a competitive marketplace that's responding to deep needs. I'd like to think these critics are right. America would be blessed if high-cost churches were evidencing a demand, perhaps a growing one, for truly challenging religious experiences. If such a demand is real, then maybe it can be cultivated into a wider cultural phenomenon that encompasses more than a few idiosyncratic communities.

I'm not convinced, however, that high-cost churches are shaping hearts as they're called to do. I suspect that they often attract people who like to feel righteous and aren't necessarily open to the kind of envelope-pushing spirituality that Jesus models. Even in high-cost churches, people flock to settings where they're among their own kind, such as self-selected small groups based on race or affinity. In such settings, others voice support for their values and lifestyles, which makes them feel more righteous than they would in settings where people actively question one another's choices. These churches, which create cultural refuges, may not be as high-cost as they appear.

I'm also not sure that tithing, fruitful as it can be, is sufficient to move the heart to a new place where lofty desires displace primitive ones. Giving money is easier, even for people who don't have a lot of it, than giving oneself and surrendering to the will of God. What's more, tithing in a consumer context can be counterproductive if it fosters a feeling of entitlement in the giver, who's paid money and expects something in return. This is not to say there is no benefit to tithing and other high-cost behaviors. Research suggests that such behaviors create strong commitments to churches and tight bonds among members. But there's no proof that these practices alone can elevate what people care about, and that's what really counts. In any case, because high-cost churches constitute just a tiny fraction of American Protestantism, their marginal existence doesn't disprove the spreading epidemic of shallow religiosity.

Americans of diverse backgrounds can see that the Church's influence is diminishing despite bustling megachurches and expanded outreach through new media. Fifty-nine percent of Americans believe that religion's influence on American life is decreasing, according to a Pew Forum survey conducted in June 2006. The survey also shows that Americans are troubled by this reality and wish the situation were different. A full 71 percent say they want religion to have more influence on American life, while just 17 percent say they want it to have less influence.

These data suggest Americans still believe religious life can shape us into a more moral people who would bring strong values to our city-council meetings, executive suites, and myriad other settings. This belief echoes one voiced by President George Washington in his 1796 farewell address. "Let us with caution indulge the supposition that morality can be maintained without religion," Washington said. "Reason and experience both forbid us to expect that national morality can prevail in exclusion of religious principle." And yet religious principle is under fire. Ironically, it is increasingly likely to disappear in a sea of religious chatter. In order to survive, it must be salvaged by churchgoers who believe in the Church's highest calling.

PART TWO

CHAPTER 5

Redeeming Religious Consumerism

THE CHURCH HAS REACHED A CROSSROADS. BUILDING on a long tradition of religious individualism, churchgoers in the new religious marketplace have come to engage the institution as consumers with needs, wants, demands, and wish lists. They insist that their desires be satisfied, not elevated or transformed. Market-sensitive churches of all stripes have responded by reinventing themselves as dispensers of entertainment and soothing comfort. In the process, age-old tools for shaping hearts have become dulled and broken. As the Church abandons its core purpose, Americans are hard-pressed to find a living institution ready to help them cultivate strong moral character. Stakeholders now need to figure out what to do with the consumerist dynamics that have become central to the contemporary Church.

THIEVES IN THE TEMPLE

Some believe that religious consumerism is beyond redemption. These theologians, pastors, and denominational leaders argue that the Church should consist of caring relationships that aren't based on money or self-interest. They fear that "the pervasiveness of the exchange mentality might tempt us into thinking we can place God under obligation." This camp rightly regards the Church as a holy institution that ultimately answers to Christ, not markets. Adherents to this school of thought generally hope to renew the Church by reestablishing it as a market-free zone.

THESE ARE NOBLE sentiments, but they ignore the breadth of consumerism's influence over the Church. That influence has been increasing for decades, to the point that church shopping and hopping have become accepted facets of church life. The religious marketplace will not be going away anytime soon. We can't just ignore it or wish it away. We will have to work within the framework of religious consumerism and use its best attributes to bring the Church back to its mission.

Despite flaws in how religious consumerism has been practiced to date, the approach has inherent merits: it is both appealing and flexible. Americans value their newfound freedom to dabble, migrate, and experiment as they please in religious life. Megachurches have grown exponentially since the early 1990s largely because, like shopping malls and amusement parks, they serve up dozens of options to suit a range of tastes. Religious publishing has also exploded, generating hundreds more titles per year than a decade ago, in order to feed a public that's still hungry after consuming what's served at the neighborhood parish. This is not to suggest that the pick-and-choose approach to spirituality is a good thing. On the contrary, the self-guided spiritual person always runs a risk of becoming a dilettante in the absence of corrective influences. But Americans appear to value how the Church has become more intent on meeting their professed needs and wants. This suggests marketplace dynamics are likely to endure, and they warrant serious attention for that reason alone.

The market model is also so flexible as to supply reason for hope. Even though churchgoers have asked the institution for problematic things in years past, what they demand in the future could very well be different. They could use their new-found leverage as consumers to demand things that will make them better people and make the Church a character-shaping institution once again. Religious consumerism is appealing and flexible enough to potentially be a useful tool in recovering the Church's mission.

My experience leads me to believe that many people are animated by the prospect of shaping the Church for the better. I sense such a craving just about every time I mention to new acquaintances that I'm an ordained minister. They routinely want to talk at length—even if we've only just met—about what they believe or don't believe, their impressions of the Church, and so forth. More often than not, they have weighty complaints to get off their chests. They yearn to be heard at long last by the institution I represent.

The dawn of unbridled religious consumerism has at last given the emotionally bruised a chance to talk back to an institution with a reputation for sometimes being judgmental or unfair. The pent-up frustration at work here is not surprising. Research suggests that many people feel they've been disenfranchised, disappointed, or hurt emotionally by their experiences of church. Now, the tide has turned on the remnants of clerical authority, and religious consumers have the upper hand. They can often compel churches to become more casual, more tolerant, more practical in their instruction. Churchgoers' eagerness to engage and critique the Church is not a scourge but a blessing, especially if they can steer the institution to recover its core mission.

A rude awakening awaits anyone who would undo the power churchgoers have realized through their new roles as proactive consumers. Recall what I learned the hard way when I tried to fence the Communion table. Liberties, once extended, are all but impossible to take back. Churchgoers enjoy their newfound power as customers, even though clergy and denominational officials may not regard them as such. For those in the pews, being customers is a step up from being sheep. They not only have more clout than they did in years past, but they also enjoy a type of influence that's familiar to them—it's much like describing preferences to a salesperson.

Church leaders face a choice. They can engage churchgoers as the customers they have become. Or they can live with the delusion that consumerism isn't dramatically shaping the Church into a new type of institution. I believe that it is time to embrace reality and begin working to redeem the consumptive habits in religious life. It is possible that consumer dynamics might actually guide the Church back to its roots—if only consumers would come to demand what they need and what the Church profoundly has to offer.

Learning how to embrace religious consumerism as a means to higher ends will require both creativity and fidelity to the Church's core mission. The challenge at hand is to claim a few legitimate, relevant traditions—ancient and recent, religious and commercial—and deploy them in new ways to meet the needs of the twenty-first century. To do that, both laity and clergy need to recover long-overlooked aspects of their respective callings. If they rise to the challenge, the Church may once again shape people of strong character—this time with help from inspired market forces.

To revitalize the Church's core mission, laypeople will need to exercise high-minded, directive influence through today's consumer channels. This will not require inventing a new role for laypeople in the Church. Instead, it will mean re-appropriating a role that dates to the Church's earliest days—a role that has been allowed to atrophy in settings where pastors and musicians put on a show and churchgoers act as passive observers.

Whether they know it or not, Christian laypeople are heirs to an ancient tradition that entrusts them to keep the Church true to its God-given purposes. Up until the late third century, everyone in the Church was a layperson, equal before God by virtue of a saving faith in Jesus Christ. Ordinary believers bore remarkable authority over the Church community. Their most important power was the ability to restore one another and the community as a whole to right relationship with God by offering forgiveness.

These early practices of lay absolution had scriptural authority and staying power. In a lesson on how to reconcile differences, Jesus assures His disciples, "whatever you bind on earth will be bound in heaven, and whatever you loose on earth will be loosed in heaven" (Matthew 18:18). In the Letter of James, the faithful are encouraged to "confess your sins to one another, and pray for one another, so that you may be healed" (James 5:16). As late as 200 A.D., church father Irenaeus articulated the norm of the period when he assured believers, "All who are justified through Christ have the sacerdotal order" to forgive sins. Only with the rise of a clergy class later in the third century did the task of forgiving sins in Christ's name get outsourced in effect to specialists.

Since Protestants routinely try to recover the Church's purest roots, it would seem logical for modern laypersons to reclaim this tradition's overarching principle: laypersons are to be elevators of souls. In the twenty-first century, that would mean using one's influence as a church member for a purpose higher than getting one's own way.

As the ancient church became more regimented, laity played a crucial role in safeguarding the institution's integrity. They dedicated themselves to identifying wisdom and strength of character—as opposed to indulging their own whims or biases—when picking leaders. Cyprian, bishop of Carthage, explained in the third century: "the laity [ought] not associate themselves with the sacrifices of a sacrilegious priest, especially since they themselves have the power either of choosing worthy priests or of rejecting unworthy ones." The challenge for such an empowered laity, explained Origen of Alexandria in the third century, was to choose a leader on the basis of who was most "eminent." In practice, this meant laity would investigate and discuss a candidate's lifelong habits to determine whether those ways were sufficiently virtuous to shape godly hearts among his followers. Even in this ancient period, laypeople could have chosen the most likeable or easygoing candidate for the job, but they knew they had a responsibility to seek out more than good personal chemistry. They were to choose one who would push them to become more virtuous.

These ancient laypeople clearly had power to decide whom to follow, much as today's church shoppers have power to select their own leaders. If today's Christians were following the example of their spiritual ancestors, they wouldn't be inclined to flee when they feel personally challenged by a leader, ministry, or program. They would expect nothing less than a tough spiritual regimen. Yet few laypeople take up the mantle of keeper of the Church's flame in our time.

Churchgoers in present-day America appear largely unaware of any such calling. I got a sense of this when I was looking for a parish ministry position. I interviewed with about eight lay search committees at as many churches. In meeting after meeting, the priority of the assembled group was to find the best possible "fit"—that is, a pastor who would blend seamlessly into a congregation's unique culture. During the process, I fielded numerous political questions: was I a Democrat? A Republican? A believer in a "woman's right to choose"? I answered questions about what I liked to do for fun and whether I intended to get married someday. Never did I hear questions about what I would do to challenge the congregation spiritually or compel a process of reckoning with God's values and priorities. Over the course of these two-hour interviews, I consistently felt like I was trying out for the job of poster boy for the congregation. This is perhaps to be expected when laypeople understand their role as one of making themselves and their fellow parishioners happy, comfortable, and entertained. But in taking this approach, laypeople default on their higher calling. They also reinforce a status quo in which churchgoers routinely feel unchallenged and disappointed.

Laypersons have drifted from their collective responsibilities at other stages in Christian history, but Protestantism has a long tradition of stirring laypeople to be more than passive onlookers. Martin Luther, whose posting of ninety-five theses on a church door touched off the Reformation in 1517, found scriptural sanction for a "priesthood of all believers" during a period when abuses of clerical power were rife. This biblical principle meant churchgoers didn't have to rely on corrupt priests to mediate their salvation. They could rest assured that "we all have the same authority with regard to the word and the sacraments." With this reclaimed authority came the responsibility for laity to safeguard the Church's integrity.

Since Luther's day, laypersons have embraced a great deal of authority in Protestant movements. They now play an oversight role, for instance, on governing boards in Lutheranism and Anglicanism. They even preach and administer sacraments in the mainline denomination Christian Church (Disciples of Christ). Roles vary from one setting to the next, but all these structures testify to a common theme: the Church needs laypeople to perceive the Way of the Cross and guide the institution accordingly. That the Church has so often revived and reaffirmed this critical role should be encouraging for communities where laypeople have, at least for the moment, lost sight of the need for sacrifice.

A redeemed religious consumerism has a salient precursor in Protestant movements that have relied upon the laity to discern God's will. Early Congregationalists, like the present-day Society of Friends (Quakers), understood consensus among ordinary church members as a sign of God's presence and blessing. They would sometimes fast and pray for an entire day until unity among the saints emerged as a sign of God's will revealed in important decisions. These practices traced their impetus to Scripture, which testifies that the Holy Spirit was present among believers when "the whole group of those who believed were of one heart and soul" (Acts 4:32). In this model, individual voices are taken seriously—so seriously that one contrarian can derail an entire congregation's plans. At the same time, personal preferences don't become tyrannical because the consensus system keeps slight majorities from dominating. Individuals in these systems are expected to advocate for agendas loftier than prioritizing their favorite hymns, charities, or social events. Having listened for the Word of God in Scripture, in prayer, and in communal reflection, they're trusted to be vocal—proactive consumers, in a sense—in demanding that which will bring out the best in one another. The key, it seems, is for churchgoers to be committed to the Church's mission of saving souls.

In America, a lay-led renewal movement would build on tradition. Throughout U.S. history, laypeople from many a denomination have challenged the Church to tackle tough, new challenges. They led the way, for instance, in developing Sunday-school lessons for a wide range of children, not just their own kids, in the nineteenth century. Laypeople launched such institutions as the Young Men's Christian Association (YMCA) and Young Women's Christian Association (YWCA), both of which aimed to shape admirable character in young people. Women-led humanitarian organizations, such as the American Red Cross (1881) and Chicago's Hull House (1889), were born as laywomen felt empowered to take risks and carry out God's will. In these movements, laypeople didn't look to the Church as an entity primarily designed to make them feel happy or fulfilled. Rather, they engaged the Church as a vessel for living out the implications of their salvation. That often meant grappling with societal needs that went unaddressed by other institutions.

A similar vision could take hold in our time as religious consumers recognize new possibilities. Perhaps they'll discover how magnanimous their demands upon the institution could be.

Today's churchgoers, of course, understand themselves as more than heirs to a religious legacy. In their lives outside of church, they're consumers of a wide range of items, from laundry detergents to landscaping services. Deciding what to buy and where to get it often involves considerations beyond price and convenience. From their conscientious shopping experiences, consumers might learn things that would help them approach their spiritual lives and religious institutions more constructively.

Today's enlightened consumer considers not only the personal benefits but also the societal and environmental repercussions of every purchase. In 2005, consumers internationally spent the equivalent of $1.6 billion on coffee, sugar, and other products bearing a "Fair Trade" label, which signals that farmers in the supply chain used eco-friendly practices and were paid a living wage. Foresters, eager to reach customers who care about habitat protection, among other issues, have in the past decade attained certification for millions of acres in order to sell their wood to producers of premium paper, lumber, and other products that bear best-practice seals. More and more investors have learned to make their conscientious voices heard in capital markets. Socially responsible mutual funds, where individuals and companies invest in firms that meet particular social or environmental criteria, have grown from being a fringe concept in the early 1970s to a $2 trillion industry today.

This kind of conscientious consumption empowers consumers to do more than contract for particular goods and services. They're leveraging their clout to shape the policies and practices of organizations, even entire industries. If this approach can take root in the hard-nosed world of business, then it probably has even more promise for shaping the Church, where decision making with more than self-interest in mind is already an accepted ideal. In fact, congregations in at least eight Protestant denominations already encourage their people to use Fair Trade products as a means of bearing witness to the Gospel and advancing justice. Churchgoers, it seems, are primed to take the next step: to steer the Church back to its character-shaping mission by choosing religious goods and services with that mission in mind.

Succeeding in this effort will involve conscientious consumption at a level not yet seen in secular markets. That's because the Church, unlike makers of gourmet coffees or chocolate bars, has an inherent mission to elevate (not just satisfy) its customers' desires. In the religious marketplace, consumers *themselves*—not a faraway company or industry—are what needs reforming. To that end, conscientious consumers should positively cry out for mission activities, classes, sermons, and other tools of the Church to be structured in ways that will lead them—the customers—to expand their hearts. Churchgoers should favor ministries that advance this most important of goals, just as other types of conscientious consumers reward companies that reduce pollution, support poor farmers, or employ disadvantaged people.

This approach to conscientious consumption might require some broadened thinking about what kind of influence responsible consumers can have. After all, even the greenest of L.L.Bean shoppers doesn't expect a retailer to help elevate what he or she wants in a product or in a retailer. But that's precisely how consumers should think of their church: as a force that's acting responsibly when it helps them to want and care about higher things. Churchgoers ought to relish this challenge—that is, to use their influence as consumers toward the end of being influenced for the better—in part because they profess to belong to something greater than an ordinary business enterprise. They have a chance to put that ethic into action for the benefit of present and future generations.

Laypersons need not negotiate this new terrain alone. Clergy can explicitly remind the laity of their ability and calling to shape the Church through their demands and offer guidance in how they might do that. Pastors can also set an example to illustrate what it means to let one's desires be reformed. And pastors can help elicit lay demands for heart-shaping experiences, much as a grocery-store manager uses product placement, advertising, and other tools of the trade to influence whether or not shoppers lunge for nutritious vegetables.

Pastors can inspire churchgoers by subjecting themselves to difficult personal challenges in their day-to-day work. Too often pastors refuse to do certain forms of ministry, such as visiting elderly shut-ins, on the grounds that "it's not my gift." That's preacher-speak for "I find it difficult" or "I don't like it." Instead of sticking with tasks that come easily to them, pastors should acknowledge these areas of personal challenge and spend time doing activities that require them to broaden themselves. This would inspire others to engage in heart-expanding behavior as well.

Pastors should expect their partners in ministry to encourage them to do good works that they find intimidating on a personal level. Anything from teen ministry to homeless outreach could make an individual pastor uncomfortable. A wise leader would seek personalized guidance in doing this hard, important work. A bishop, board of deacons, or spiritual director, for instance, would welcome a pastor's plea for gentle prodding in directions where a hardened heart stands in the way. With encouragement, pastors would systematically face their fears. They would in turn bring to the pulpit many an edifying anecdote to illustrate how hearts can be changed under difficult circumstances. This would be common practice in a church where pastors believe their own hearts need elevating.

In terms of seeking out personal challenges, pastors-in-training might serve as a better example than settled pastors.

This was true in my case. As a ministry intern, I learned from a couple of wise mentors to dwell in precisely those situations that initially made me want to run. They believed I'd learn patience and compassion, qualities that would serve me well in ministry. With trepidation, I agreed to try.

In a blighted section of Bridgeport, Connecticut, I twice a month visited an immobile elderly woman in a dark, unventilated room where she lived virtually all her days. My supervisor warned me: it smells like feces in her house because she finds it hard to clean up after her dogs. Not even in my pizza-delivering days as a teenager had I ever been in such an unhygienic home. The air was nauseating. Sometimes we'd chat; sometimes I'd remove a few droppings with her permission. But most of the time, I simply shared her environment for a little while in an effort to convey that she was loved and dignified, no matter her circumstances. In a small way, this humbling visitation taught me to care about an invisible segment of society that I had previously been quite content to ignore. The experience gave me stamina, even passion, for visiting elders who lived in dark or downright scary homes. When I would speak to groups and mention this work, others would talk about how they too might bear witness to God's ways by doing more of what they find difficult. My mentors were right: exhibiting God's love under revolting conditions had in fact made me more compassionate and courageous.

Some of this disquieting spiritual formation brought me face-to-face with groups I had previously tried to avoid. As a ministry intern in suburban Unionville, Connecticut, for instance, I led a teenage youth group that warily viewed me as an authority figure. I dreaded making painfully awkward small talk about clothing labels and other things that held no interest for me. But in hindsight, I realize how elevating it was for me to forge authentic connections with that gangly group. We drummed together, for instance, with open palms on any surface we could find because we could all appreciate a good, table-tapping groove. We laughed together about the kinds of food we couldn't stand. I learned to speak of faith in concrete images, a skill Jesus had in abundance, but one that had eluded me personally in my Yale theology classes. These teens put so much effort into collection drives for needy kids that they gave me a clear image of compassion in action. Somehow we came to care about each other, enough to stay in touch in a couple of cases, even though in the beginning we hadn't seemed to have anything in common.

Once I'd settled into ministry, however, these types of challenges became rarer. I was no longer required to bond with teens in my new congregation. Some members of the congregation wisely urged me to get involved with the youth group, but I didn't recognize their encouragement as the healthy spiritual challenge that it was. Because I didn't ask mentors or committees to push me out of my comfort zones, stagnation set in. I didn't get to know individuals who depended on our food-pantry collections because I didn't have to and no one suggested that I should. I'm sure our food-collecting ministry languished in part because I couldn't bring actual faces or life circumstances to mind when making appeals for donations. In hindsight, I see how I needed guides to help me identify where my heart had hardened and to develop a method—difficult spiritual exercises, perhaps—to soften it. Had I taken such proactive steps, I would have set a better example for a community that looked to me for cues and encouragement.

Pastors have more to offer than lessons gleaned from their own spiritual formation. Since many enter ministry as a second career, they often bring a lot of know-how from the business world. That could be an asset when trying to tap a new marketplace's full potential.

Pastors steeped in the ways of business can shape lofty desires in their clientele. Anyone who's been a manager, for instance, knows that employees and customers are more likely to take advantage of programs if they're promoted and encouraged by people in leadership positions. Whether an organizational initiative succeeds or fails often depends largely on whether a manager supports it with words, time, and effort. In the Church, clergy have a lot of sway in determining whether particular ideas ever become actual ministries. Church leaders can develop and support programs that help churchgoers cultivate virtue. Meditative prayer groups, for example, submit to a discipline that involves resisting temptations to chatter or to let the mind race from one subject to the next. In the process, they learn to quiet their minds and stimulate regions of the brain associated with empathy. Over time, they become more aware of and concerned for others' needs. They become more Christ-like. Other activities that push the comfort zones of congregants, such as prison ministries, can serve a similar purpose by teaching churchgoers to care for people who can seem hard to love. By identifying which ministries and devotional practices actually expand human capacities to reflect God's love, pastors can begin to focus on those most worthy of vigorous support.

Pastors have many tools to boost interest in such ministries. They can invite testimonies during worship from those who've changed for the better by pursuing a hard path that they didn't want to take. They can document highly challenging ministries and share these stories in sermons, Web sites, newsletters, and other media. They can reward challenge-seekers by giving them personal attention and asking questions to shed light on the fruits of their experiences. Just as doctors can motivate healthy behaviors by sharing research or recounting success stories, clergy have myriad tools to stoke cravings for experiences that shape virtue. They just need to use them.

Church leaders also raise the bar for religious consumerism when they revamp how to measure progress in ministry. One congregation where I worked during seminary had an unfortunately typical, albeit often unspoken, standard: members fired one of their pastors for failing to bring in more people and more money. Membership levels had been flat during his tenure, and donations had slipped slightly. When angry parish-

ioners criticized him at a congregational meeting, their com-
ments were met with nods and applause. The pastor was gone
within weeks. Those who hold exclusively to such a standard
have lost track of the crucial fact the Church doesn't exist, as
some businesses do, for the purpose of growing numerically.
Clergy need to remind parishioners that the organization exists
to save souls, which can be a painful process. Some attrition
should be expected as a cost of being faithful to the Church's
mission and making difficult demands of its members.

Pastors need to rethink how they measure success and
progress. The Church does not need to grow constantly in
terms of attendance and revenues, and pastors should trust that
the Lord will provide for their organization's needs as long as
the Church stays true to its core mission. Instead of counting
heads and dollars, they should be tracking how well people are
growing—are their hearts broadening? Are they manifesting
sacrificial love? Clergy and laypeople alike could embrace those
standards for evaluating whether a ministry is succeeding.
When Christians actively seek out experiences to help them become more virtuous, then religious consumerism is surely
working to the good.

Pastors can also expand their repertoires by tapping into
new scientific insights. Studies based on thousands of brain
scans, for instance, show that certain prayer techniques increase
social awareness and compassion. Other research on brain
chemistry has found that people are more likely to make selfless
decisions when the hormone oxytocin is activated. Researchers

hope to know more soon about which behaviors elicit or muffle the production of oxytocin—valuable information for those who hope to inspire large-heartedness in others. The Dalai Lama Center for Compassion and Altruism Research and Education at Stanford University is using brain imaging to explore such issues as why some children become bullies and how parents can increase their own compassion. Pastors owe it to their congregations to be up to date on the latest findings in their field—that is, the craft of refining what human beings value. Staying current and putting these insights to work in ministry settings would reinforce the message that shaping hearts is a congregational priority. It would also help inspire religious consumers to seek out what the Church has to offer, through ancient as well as brand-new techniques.

Though pastors have the tools to encourage higher-level consumerism, they must be wary of using these tools counterproductively. Even Christian doctrine can have a detrimental effect when it's misused. In preaching about grace, the unearned divine gift that enables salvation, Christians must not imply that grace makes personal sacrifice unimportant. It is easy for churchgoers to believe, wrongly, that their lives can be as indulgent as they like because Christ's sacrifice on the Cross was sufficient for their redemption. To live by such an ethic is to reveal a lack of faith, since faith involves confidence in God's challenging ways. No pastor wants a flock where faith is in short supply, but that's what pastors get when they suggest that grace is a free pass.

Pastors need to accept some of the blame when their congregants' lives prove every bit as materialistic and self-centered as those of their nonbelieving neighbors. They need to ask themselves: have I led people to believe grace is cheaper than it really is? Have my people learned from my theological emphases that personal sacrifice in the name of God is pointless? If they have, then they're living by a spiritually deadly message, even if it is cloaked in the veneer of orthodoxy. Pastors need to be sure they're not only proclaiming orthodox doctrine, but are also spelling out its broad requirements for the Christian life. This latter step is the one that ruffles feathers in pews and makes preachers vulnerable to charges of hypocrisy. But pastors who don't do it contribute to religious consumerism's devolution into a purely self-indulgent enterprise.

Though they will play different roles in redeeming religious consumerism, laity and clergy need to embrace a common vision for the twenty-first-century Church. The vision must involve institutionalizing practices that elevate members' personal desires. The Church has a long tradition of asceticism to serve just this purpose. It deserves to be recovered and perhaps even reinvented to address today's crisis in personal character and usher in a new era of enlightened religious consumerism.

Asceticism refers to lifestyles marked by abstinence from certain worldly pleasures. It has been a valuable tool for helping Christians reform and elevate desires since ancient times. Men and women withdrew in the second century to the

Egyptian desert to endure solitude, extensive fasting, and little sleep. The goal was always to contemplate God with a pure mind. Their logic, informed by Greek philosophy as well as Christ's example, held that bodily cravings, when indulged, soon return with an even greater vengeance. They cause blindness to all but instinctual passions, thus reducing man to a primitive state and making him oblivious to the higher, selflessly loving ways of God. Early Christians believed that these cravings could be subdued and diminished over time through learned habits of self-restraint. The concept begat monasteries and convents, where monks and nuns have for nearly two millennia modeled a Christian ideal by practicing celibacy and focusing on God in prayer. It led to the celibate priesthood in Catholicism and reinforced monogamy, or abstinence from multiple sexual partners, in Christian marriage. Enduring practices in certain strains of Protestantism to shun food, dancing, fancy clothes, and jewelry can be traced back to a belief that asceticism can change and elevate how human beings experience desire.

Although ascetic practices can do a great deal to redeem religious consumerism, contemporary Christians will need to create new forms of asceticism for today's world. That's because some past forms can seem detached from any useful purpose and even dangerous. In ancient days, when "mortifying" the flesh entailed blessedness, heroes of the faith sometimes took the convention to extremes. One sat atop a pole for weeks. Others donned hair shirts by day, or rested their heads on wooden pillows by night. These practices, intended to show solidarity with a suffering Christ and to build spiritual strength, offer little to modern sensibilities. They seem foolish, pointless, and potentially harmful.

Yet just as flawed elections don't erase the merits of democracy, questionable expressions of asceticism don't negate the value of this broad and still-evolving tradition. I know from experience that the desire to smoke really does dissipate with cessation of the habit. Shopaholics help themselves when they stay away from malls and let phone calls from their shopping buddies go to voice mail. Asceticism has much to offer a generation that's become enslaved to low desires, but only if believers adopt ascetic practices that speak uniquely to the spiritual needs of the present age.

Skeptics are sure to scoff at the notion of American Christians abstaining from worldly pleasures. Too late, they'll say. Americans have become suspicious of any faith-based lifestyles that involve substantial sacrifice. Many of the fastest-growing congregations in America teach that God wants Christians to be rich. Churchgoers in this country routinely see faith as an avenue to abundance, not self-denial. An ascetic label in America's spiritual supermarket wouldn't sell, the argument goes, because Americans see no value in self-deprivation.

This skeptical argument doesn't give American Christians enough credit. Americans are no strangers to sacrifice. They work hard and delay gratification to pursue any number of good things, from a stable career to a home for one's family.

Many don't even take the full two weeks of annual vacation to which they're entitled. The idea of self-denial for the sake of a higher goal isn't as foreign as some observers might suggest. What's more, many American Christians take their faith very seriously. They're far more observant than their counterparts in other Western nations. American Protestants are heirs to a dynamic tradition of revivalism, which cyclically brings people back to their roots of exuberant worship and inspired personal sacrifice. These factors together suggest that American Christians just might start demanding guidance in the ascetic life. Perhaps all that's missing is a spark to get the fire going.

In some corners of America, asceticism is already resurgent, though not necessarily in religious packaging. Environmentalists are claiming the ascetic tradition in order to hone habits that may help save an imperiled Earth. I've interviewed middle-aged, financially comfortable women who refuse to turn on an air conditioner, even when the mercury reads 100, in a self-denying bid to fight global warming. I've talked with Boston-area hikers who say they can't morally justify the carbon emissions for a three-hour drive to New Hampshire's White Mountains. I've heard eco-conscious undergraduates at the University of Vermont proudly tell of leaving the heat off in their apartments even when outdoor temperatures drop to a dangerous 20 degrees below zero. Just a few years ago, such practices would have seemed ridiculous, and to some they still do—but such is always the way with asceticism. A sense of urgency to avert an apocalyptic outcome (in this case, an environmental catastrophe) is compelling those with higher yearnings to adopt voluntary restraints. The ascetic giant that always lurks in the human soul is once again waking up in America—albeit in a largely secular, green outfit.

To expect consumers of any stripe—religious or otherwise—to ask for hardship isn't as unrealistic as it might seem. There's solid precedent for it in the secular marketplace. Consider music students. In shopping around for great instructors, they don't browse as they would at Costco—that is, they don't search out the teacher who will give the most payoff in return for the least sacrifice. They look instead for a knowledgeable guide who will push them to maximize their abilities. The process, they know, will be uncomfortable. Fingers will ache after endless scales and arpeggios. Fun opportunities will pass them by as they explain to friends, "Sorry, I need to practice." They're aware that only through sacrifice will they develop their talents in accordance with their abilities. Athletes consume coaching services in a similar way. An aspiring gymnast, swimmer, or tennis star wants the coach who will make him or her work hard, endure discomfort as necessary, and achieve hard-to-reach goals.

Consumers of this ilk hunger for something higher than indulgence of their primitive appetites. They yearn to develop mastery through discipline and are willing to subject themselves to challenging regimens in order to reach their goals. Not all consumers always want to get as much and give as little as possible. A certain type of consumer reaches higher, and religious consumers could soon become part of this category.

Churchgoers could approach religious experience in much the same way as a musician or athlete seeks training. They could bring an ascetic sensibility to the project of seeking God. Instead of seeking out the most entertaining or comforting church, they might look for preachers who will take them out of their comfort zones, or outreach ministries that will shatter their preconceptions. Congregations could vary widely in how they accommodate or stoke demands for heart-stretching experiences. In one setting, a panel of elders might meet with individuals and customize regimens, such as daily centering prayer for the restless and overly talkative, or weekly soup-kitchen service for the elite professional. Elsewhere an entire congregation might agree to live by a certain code, such as following a vegetarian diet for moral reasons. Or a church might brainstorm about which types of ministries would positively challenge its members—teaching English to immigrant neighbors? Visiting hospital patients with HIV/AIDS? Leading spiritual sing-alongs in nursing homes? A group might launch a set of reasonable initiatives, encourage members to do those that scare them most, and then discuss over a monthly dinner how they've grown and changed. Ministry structures for offering encouragement could vary as widely as the ascetic practices. As long as participants' hearts are reformed by rigorous discipline, the Church will be on track to be what the world needs it to be: an impactful training ground for souls.

In redeeming religious consumption through a new asceticism, the Church would need to be cautious of certain pitfalls. Safeguards would need to be put in place to ensure that individuals don't glorify suffering for its own sake or go to such extremes that they endanger themselves or anyone else. Since asceticism by definition involves willful self-deprivation, one always needs to remember that more of the ascetic way isn't always better for spiritual growth. In excess, it can become masochistic and counterproductive. Organizers must keep in mind that only a measure of discomfort is needed to stretch hearts, and maximizing hardship is never the goal. With healthy guidelines, individuals need not fear an ascetic approach to faith.

Churches will also need to guard against the risks of legalism, a seductive way of thinking in which people wrongly believe that salvation hinges on adherence to a specific set of behaviors. Legalism can lead to the spiritual sickness of self-righteousness and undermine all else that the Church tries to do. To guard against it, participants in ascetic practices will need to convey vigilantly and often that what they do is a response to God's grace, not an attempt to earn divine favor. Churches that design safeguards appropriate to their local contexts should be able to offer the blessings of asceticism without getting dragged down by wayward applications of it.

To be sure, not everyone will be convinced that the Church needs a new ethic of asceticism. Some find ascetic practice inherently objectionable on philosophical grounds. Certain strains of feminism, for instance, worry that women too often tolerate abusive circumstances as a consequence of believing that God values voluntary self-denial. Thinkers in those movements might worry about any situation where someone is encouraged to live a sacrificial lifestyle. And of course those who embrace faith as a path to material wealth and comfort will not be easily convinced, either.

If critics simply decline to participate in renewal of Christian asceticism, then that decision should be respected. But if critics argue that the Church shouldn't be allowed to offer more proactive guidance in a sacrificial way of faith, then believers need to push back for the sake of the institution and the society they love. When the Church is stripped of its ability to compel a higher way, it becomes a handmaiden to a culture where greed and hedonism go unchecked. No other institution will fill the void. Christians must insist that the Church has a right to engage its people proactively with a goal of elevating concerns and desires. On that basis, renewal can begin.

Spiritual decay is rife in the American Church largely because the institution has lost touch with the way Jesus makes disciples. His Way is to accept all types, build people up and assign them tough challenges. To a woman spared punishment for adultery, he instructs: "Go—and sin no more" (John 8:11). He calls fishermen away from their livelihoods and sends them where "men will hand you over to the councils and flog you" (Matthew 10:17). He says each follower should "deny himself and take up his cross and follow me. For whoever wants to save his life will lose it, but whoever loses his life for me will find it" (Matthew 16:24–25). A more ascetic religious consumerism would create true-to-the-cross pathways for those who crave to know the Lord but find the route overgrown and unmarked in today's Church. Such paths are worth recovering, even if skeptics don't take part.

CHAPTER 6

Signs of Hope in the
New Religious Marketplace

IN THE EARLY 2000S, GINNY SCHRENKLER WAS ENJOYING the American dream with a good job and a nice house in suburban Oakdale, Minnesota, when her concerns for comfort and security started giving way to a higher calling. Sermons she heard at Woodland Hills Church called for disciples to model a new social order, where racial boundaries would fall, the weak would be honored, and outcasts would be embraced. She began to wonder: what can I do to realize this vision of God's Kingdom?

Schrenkler began tutoring African American children in St. Paul's inner city as a volunteer on Tuesday nights. As she continued to listen for her calling at church, she met others who had moved from an affluent suburb to an urban, mostly African American neighborhood in order to bridge a cultural divide. In 2005, she took a radical step. She sold her Oakdale home, bought an inner-city property, and put down roots in an area known for graffiti, break-ins, and a constant struggle to survive.

Three years later, she had no regrets. At age thirty-six, Schrenkler had become an aunt-like friend to lots of African American kids in her neighborhood. During the week we met, she treated a group of children to an impromptu after-school brownie-baking session in her kitchen. Still, the transition hasn't been easy. She gets interrupted by spontaneous visits from neighborhood schoolchildren even on her busy days. Her new home's value isn't likely to appreciate soon, if ever, what with the abandoned structures and littered lots looming large nearby. But she is at peace with the costs she's incurred for a higher purpose. "It's not as safe here as Oakdale, but I didn't know my neighbors there," she said. "Here, God has given me a family that cares about me."

Schrenkler's experience isn't typical, but it nonetheless points to what is possible in an age of religious consumerism. It shows that a competitive religious marketplace can produce experiences that broaden a person's range of concerns and motivate sacrificial, rewarding choices. As she sought out fellowship with people who shared her values, she found some who didn't blithely affirm her comfortable lifestyle but instead helped her choose a riskier, more challenging pathway. Her story suggests that, under the right conditions, equally profound experiences could unfold elsewhere.

I met Schrenkler in October 2008 as I set out on a mission. I wanted to see where and how the Church is effectively shaping hearts in twenty-first-century America. This search for insight led me to metropolitan Minneapolis/St. Paul, where I observed practices and conducted interviews at four Christian institutions: Woodland Hills Church, Abbey Way Covenant Church, Eagle Brook Church, and Augsburg College. Lessons learned in the Twin Cities, I figured, could be instructive elsewhere. A medium-sized metropolitan area, Minneapolis/St. Paul is no huge metropolis with unique dynamics. What works there could likely be applied to churches and communities elsewhere. The Twin Cities are also a consumerist mecca. The area proudly claims the nation's largest mall as well as myriad shopping centers and subdivisions carved out of former farmland. If any place has to grapple with a pervasive consumer mind-set, this one does.

In Minneapolis/St. Paul, religion is a highly competitive industry. Scores of Lutheran churches compete with hungry, up-and-coming evangelical ones while still other denominations vie for the loyalties of transient churchgoers. Christians who opt for challenging forms of discipleship do so despite an abundance of cushier alternatives. Whatever is compelling Christians to reach higher in metropolitan Minneapolis, I thought, might help spark similar movement elsewhere.

I used two basic criteria in selecting the four institutions I examined. Each showed sensitivity to market demand, and each was inspiring clientele to tackle difficult challenges. In addition,

I sought diversity in terms of attendance totals, denominational affiliation, theological emphases (liberal vs. conservative), and location (urban vs. suburban). Across this broad spectrum, it seemed, desires were being reformed and elevated even as the marketplace churned.

Though no silver-bullet formula materialized, three elements set these institutions apart from those where affirmation abounds and challenge is rare. All intentionally reinforce the notion that spiritual growth is supposed to be difficult and uncomfortable at times. They also have structures in place to get their congregants thinking about the costs and joys that their peers experience by following faith paths that aren't always easy. And they have mechanisms for compelling individuals to face fears and engage in practices that stretch their hearts in necessary directions. How these institutions express these features varies enormously, and not one of them has perfected the enterprise. But each testifies in a unique way to what is attainable when a church takes advantage of the dynamics of the new religious marketplace.

For a megachurch, Woodland Hills Church in Maplewood, Minnesota, keeps a very low profile. When I arrived on a Sunday morning, I saw not a single sign identifying the church—just an unmarked, sprawling building that once housed a Home Depot. The nondescript veneer is intentional, pastor Greg Boyd later told me, because the church isn't aiming to grow its ranks as much as possible. Rather, it's aiming to manifest the Kingdom of God, and that entails pushing people beyond their comfort zones.

After a few praise songs and a presentation by a missionary to Mozambique, Boyd wasted no time making the crowd uncomfortable. He read from the blog of a girl who attends Woodland Hills and who is confined to a wheelchair. She described how painful it is to sense that everyone, in church as elsewhere, feels entitled to gawk at her deformity for as long as they please. "It's the kind of stare that you give when you're looking at a car crash," he read from her entry, "filled with curiosity and the gratitude that it's not your problem." He used this devastating blog entry to point out just how far the Church needs to go in order to reflect Jesus, who loved outcasts and welcomed them into his fold. Some members of the congregation fidgeted uncomfortably in their folding chairs. Others dabbed tears. Nobody appeared the least bit comforted or entertained. But they listened, and left with a concrete challenge from their pastor: to add at least one social outcast to their inner circles of friends.

Worship doesn't always go so smoothly at Woodland Hills. Boyd says people get up and walk out during sermons, in protest of what they're hearing, at least a couple times per month. By 2008, average attendance had dropped to about 3,000 from a peak of 5,000 four years earlier, when Boyd refused to champion elements of the GOP platform or otherwise mix politics with worship. Yet because the church has no fancy light-and-sound show to maintain and keeps overhead low, finances remain solid and staffers don't feel pressured to water down their principled statements.

"There's none of that consumer stuff in the New Testament," Boyd told me in an interview in his St. Paul living room. "Jesus says, 'If you want to follow me, then take up your cross.' It's a hard saying. And most people don't want that—or they think they don't want that—so they go away."

To encourage costly discipleship, Woodland Hills showcases stories of congregants who've taken risks and realized extraordinary outcomes. This tactic came through at a retreat for about fifty small-group leaders. The afternoon consisted of testimonies from people who had taken big risks for the sake of the Gospel and reaped joyful rewards. Church member Sandra Unger and her husband, Dave, told how they'd left a safe, suburban home and resettled in St. Paul's inner city. Beside them, five African American friends from their neighborhood told how they came to trust the Ungers, who were in some cases the first white friends they'd ever had. Teenager Wesley Egan said the Ungers welcomed him and his friends with late-night snacks and conversation when home life got too chaotic to bear. Dee Hampton saw the Ungers as trustworthy after they brought her teenage son, Ricky, to a hospital when he'd been in a street fight. Bonds grew so tight over a few years that Ms. Hampton's teenage boys would sometimes live with the Ungers for a few months at a time. These uncommon tales of close friendship between black teens and a middle-aged white couple underscored a message for the small-group leaders to take away:

amazing things can happen when a Gospel vision inspires risk and sacrifice.

"I love these people," Ms. Hampton said of the Ungers. "I can't even imagine growing old and not being able to pick up the phone and call Sandra. I know that until I leave this Earth, these people are going to be in my life."

Small-group leaders learned that these sentiments were hard earned. The Ungers told of their costs, such as pouring their savings into blighted real estate instead of property with a better chance of appreciating in value. Black and white panelists told how friends thought they were crazy and shunned them for crossing racial boundaries. But they also spoke of the peace that comes with following Jesus' costly path. "This is the Kingdom," Sandra Unger told the group. "It's going to cost us something. It's not easy. But it's worth it."

The all-white crowd was inspired. The room brimmed with energy as people asked questions about the keys to transcending racial and class boundaries. They got tips on how to do cross-cultural ministry from the African Americans on the panel: Be sincere. Come to learn, not to rescue. Be patient because trust takes time. They also received assurance that relocating to the inner city or focusing on interracial bridge building *isn't* a calling for everyone. Leaders walked away with stories to motivate members of the church's forty-one small groups. Within days, the lay leaders would be recounting for their small groups the blessings they'd heard about. They'd be asking group members how they might follow similarly costly and rewarding paths. Those churchgoers seeking satisfaction in the spiritual life would receive concrete examples of how to take up one's cross and follow Jesus.

"We want to give [typically consumerist churchgoers] less and less and less of what they're looking for," Boyd told me. "We're trying to create a hunger for more, but we haven't done a good job of giving them the 'more.' We have to do better at creating vibrant small-group communities where people are living out the self-sacrificial kingdom and making that attractive so that people want that."

Hearts are stretched when individuals let others compel them, in spite of their fears, to follow difficult pathways. In small groups at Woodland Hills, for instance, participants aren't expected to provide unconditional moral support for each other. Instead, leaders encourage members to let the group offer Christian counsel on a big personal decision before it's a fait accompli. For example, an individual might say he's thinking about buying a $50,000 car. The group would explore with him whether that particular use of $50,000 would help manifest God's Kingdom, where the love of God overcomes man-made divisions. Peers might suggest buying a $20,000 car and putting a portion of the leftover money toward an important cause. Such a conversation would be anathema in most of America, since few in this country ever invite groups to weigh in on their discretionary consumer choices. But Woodland Hills' groups, at least when they live up to Boyd's exhortations, strive to shape character by encouraging habits of self-denial and magnanimity. Members believe an effective small-group ministry impacts how people use money, time, and other resources. Hence they hone the habit, difficult as it may be, of seeking guidance about big life choices.

Individuals at Woodland Hills sometimes make decisions based on an ethic that says the needs of the poor are paramount. That happened when thirty-year-old Aaron Day quit his job teaching elementary students at a suburban Christian school. He agreed to a pay cut in order to become the director of youth programming at The Lift, an inner-city church and job-skills training center supported by Woodland Hills. For him, the calculus was simple: these children, who've often missed meals and come to The Lift's programs hungry, needed him more than the private-school kids did. He relocated to the tough neighborhood where the ministry is located. He's adjusting to a lower standard of living. He let the community's needs guide him onto this sacrificial path, and even though he's never been obsessed with brands or bling, he finds he's growing even less and less concerned about owning electronic gadgets, jewelry, and other non-necessities.

"You put less emphasis on stuff when you hang around with people who don't have a lot of stuff," Day says. In biblical terms, his heart is learning contentment.

The possibility of pointed, even confrontational questioning also moves the members of Woodland Hills. That's what changed everything for nineteen-year-old Cortez Warren, an African American former gang member who grew up using drugs and getting into trouble. Having seen his friends benefit from their friendships with Sandra Unger, he came to trust and open up to her, despite his family's warnings to stay away from this white woman whom they viewed warily. His life's direction changed, he says, when she asked one night about his goals. He said he hoped to own a car-repair shop that would offer affordable service for low-income people. At the time, he was gangbanging and often slept in other people's cars or in abandoned houses.

"She asked me, 'Do you think you're on track to reach that goal? Is the way you're living going to get you there?'" Warren said after worship in The Lift's rented warehouse space. "I'm a changed person because of that question and the big decisions I made afterward." He resolved to quit drugs, avoid certain former friends, and start saving for his repair shop.

These pathways of challenging one another have led to some steep personal costs. Warren's family broke off ties with him when he got involved with The Lift. Thieves have ransacked Aaron Day's car. Boyd has at times watched his church shrink from one month to the next. Everyone who listens to the church's sermons, attends challenging small groups, or serves in urban ministries feels more of the world's pain than they would in a church that specializes in entertainment and therapy.

Enduring these difficulties together gives the community a defining sense of ongoing challenge. Churchgoers understand that, as Boyd says, "To get your deepest need met—the one you may not even know you have—you first have to crucify your-self." Boyd admits that many church members may have a long way to go before they accept costly discipleship in their day-to-day lives. But if they miss the mark, it won't be for lack of op-portunity or encouragement.

At the other end of the spectrum as far as size is concerned, Abbey Way Covenant Church works without the resources or scale of a megachurch. The community exemplifies "New Monasticism," a movement that aims to deepen Christian spir-ituality by incorporating monastic practices into ordinary peo-ple's lives. A four-year-old congregation affiliated with the Evangelical Covenant Church, Abbey Way counts just sixty members, half of whom are children. They're mostly white and highly educated, with lots of teachers and scholars in the ranks. Intimate relationships among members provide the basis for their ministry.

Abbey Way sets expectations high by looking to monks and nuns as role models. Members follow a code based on the 1,500-year-old Rule of St. Benedict, which has through the ages guided monks and others in how to live a godly life in community. The necessary commitments here are fourfold: an-cient prayers at set times of the day; monthly spiritual direc-tion, a practice that involves discerning God's movement in one's life with the help of others; biweekly chapter meetings, which bring five or so families together to relate life stories, forge close bonds, and discern God's call for Abbey Way; and gatherings every Sunday in the congregation's rented space at a Minneapolis Baptist church for a potluck meal and worship from 4 to 7:30 p.m. Beyond these four major codes, the group's long-term vision involves relocating members to a neighborhood where the group feels called to address existing social problems. They may find individual homes in the neighborhood or move into a shared building together.

Abbey Way's members are hungry to share their lives with one another on a level that is inconceivable in most U.S. churches today. Larry Houk, for instance, says relationships forged at Abbey Way are like those of the rural church community that embraced him as a youth growing up on a Minnesota farm. Bob and Jan Bros have wandered from their Roman Catholic roots, but they're still drawn to the insights that monks and nuns seem to hone through their sacrificial, highly structured lives. Many members of Abbey Way first developed their cravings for a shared, tight-knit Christian life while attending a megachurch that felt too consumerist and left them wanting more. They've created a pioneering community to meet their own demand for a Christian life that is made meaningful in part through its rigor. In this, they demonstrate the religious marketplace's capacity to both meet demands and shape character through substantial challenges.

Giving up certain aspects of religious consumerism is part of the challenge of Abbey Way membership. Because members must commit for a year at a time and revisit their commitments annually, quitting the community after a tiff is not an option.

Churchgoers need to muster the maturity, courage, and humility to work out their differences and remain on intimate terms. These norms diverge from those of most churches, where it's increasingly rare for attendees to become members at all and the right to flee at any time is a fact of life. Yet even forfeiting the power to run away satisfies a demand of the typical Abbey Way member.

"I learned from the nuns that there was something about following Jesus that was beyond normal life," says Jan Bros, pastor of Abbey Way. "There is some kind of lifestyle change and sacrifice involved.... If it's truly going to be a transformational experience, there has to be something that holds you there, following Jesus in community. That's where we're forced to get beyond 'this is what I want' and allow the Spirit of God to change us."

In same-sex spiritual direction groups, Abbey Way members grow by making themselves vulnerable and bearing one another's pain. One person talks about his life's challenges while others listen. Then, after a few minutes of quiet reflection, the speaker sits silently while others take turns saying where God's hand might be moving in his or her life. The process can be grueling. When I visited the men's meeting in a law-office conference room on a Saturday morning, the five group members were visibly pained to hear of one another's struggles. They wiped sweaty brows, buried faces in their hands, and squirmed uneasily in their seats. They took turns confessing inadequate efforts to support beleaguered wives, to mend strained familial relationships, and to cope with stresses. One case involved a career-ending and marriage-threatening brain injury. This was not anyone's idea of a fun Saturday morning. But they pressed ahead nonetheless to fulfill a higher calling to be introspective and forthright.

"It's so hard to bring this up," said Brian Toutge as he talked about his wife, Tonya's, church-related stress. "I don't want it to sound like we don't want to be doing Abbey Way, because we do. But Tonya is up until 2 or 2:30 every morning with work and church stuff. There's a lot that could be picked up by others at Abbey Way, but nobody else is doing it.... Her legs are starting to buckle."

Two days later at the women's spiritual-direction group, Tonya Toutge shared her burden in Ardie Gallant's candle-lit living room. She told how her daughter was suffering daily anxiety attacks so severe that she didn't ever want to go to school. She spoke of her workload as a professor and volunteer organizer who keeps Abbey Way functioning from week to week. Fighting back tears, she said, "It amazes me that I haven't imploded." But neither of the two others in the group gave her a hug. Neither one suggested ways to lighten her load. There was no rush to relieve her pain. They instead waited in silence for about five minutes and then reminded her that God gives His chosen ones hard tasks.

"Moses was overwhelmed, and he did just fine," Ms. Gallant calmly told her. "Peter was overwhelmed, but only when he took his eyes off Jesus."

Tonya wasn't surprised or offended by their response. She felt loved, as long hugs exchanged after the session could attest. On her way out the door, she smiled and summed up an ethic of the church: "We're committed to not avoiding pain."

In less structured situations, Abbey Way members continue to challenge one another to make sacrificial commitments. For example, Heather and Douglas Dart teamed up with another couple to paint both families' homes during summer 2008. None of the four adults had any professional painting experience, but it seemed like a good way to build bonds and help each other in a practical manner. Benefits would come at a price—the families committed almost a whole summer's worth of weekends to the cause. But the two couples felt they were living out convictions—in this case, to share life together by sharing paintbrushes, ladders, and child care for a season.

"There were weekends when we didn't want to go paint their house, when we had other things we wanted to do, but we went anyway," Heather Dart said. "Even though it took longer this way, it was easier than it would have been to paint our house by ourselves because we [two families] were together."

When relationships get strained, Abbey Way members see opportunity for the kind of growth that God values. At one point, a parent insisted that no church-related gathering should be off-limits to kids. This made Ardie Gallant uncomfortable. She had an aversion to high-energy kids. Their noise and running made her uneasy, and she liked to be tranquil at church gatherings. Yet rather than create a church-wide tempest or part ways in a huff, she and this parent hashed out their differences and came to an understanding. They agreed that children would be welcome as long as they adhered to a code of good behavior and reasonable self-restraint. Parents agreed to make expectations clearer to their kids. Gallant found the conversations tense at times, but the experience bore precious fruit. She came to feel more comfortable around the congregation's children—so comfortable that she now doesn't hesitate to correct their behavior when they cut in line and grab for dessert. Now there's no one at the church who makes her uneasy, and her love for God's creatures is a little broader than it used to be.

Abbey Way members admit their systems have room for improvement. Sometimes people are so focused on relationships inside the church that outreach is neglected. Missions to address needs in the city have, to the frustration of some, consisted of just a few one-time efforts rather than a sustained campaign in any coherent direction. The church also lacks diversity in terms of race and professional backgrounds. Both these issues may turn out to be perennial problems, since the church is organized to focus on internal dynamics and attracts a niche consumer. But the people of Abbey Way are aware of these shortcomings and aspire to do better as their experiment progresses.

Weaknesses don't detract from Abbey Way's capacity to be an inspirational model. Church member David Olson, who directs the denomination's church-planting efforts to establish new churches, says he's never seen another church build so much trust and openness among members. He attributes much of Abbey Way's success in this area to shared rigorous commitments to expanding and elevating hearts. Trust and openness provide a solid platform for spiritual progress in the years ahead.

"What Abbey Way does really well is foster deeper levels of community," Olson said. "I've been in tons of small groups and Bible studies—all of that kind of thing—but this has really pushed it down to a much deeper level.... There's not going to be any part of my life that I would be unwilling, in the right context, to be transparent about." He paused.

"That's a heavy concept, huh?"

On the surface, it appears that the new religious marketplace has been good to Eagle Brook Church, a megachurch with three campuses in Minneapolis' northern suburbs. Since the late 1980s, the congregation has ballooned from a few hundred weekly attendees to more than 11,000. A member of the customer-friendly Willow Creek Association, Eagle Brook has thrived by offering what consumers want: a nonsectarian name, upbeat music, practical "messages" (aka sermons), a gift shop, and abundant parking.

Yet despite the church's rapid growth, Eagle Brook leaders discovered in 2008 that attendees weren't manifesting signs of real spiritual growth. A congregational survey found that fewer than one in four had become "Christ-centered Christians" who "live a sacrificial life" and strive to let God's values take priority over personal preferences. Most were more eager to be served by the church than to serve the institution or their fellow members, said pastor Bob Merritt as he presented the findings during Sunday-morning worship. Churchgoers who described themselves as "frustrated" in their faith lives frequently said the church was not helping them to "advance spiritually." These findings suggested that despite a packed house every Sunday, Eagle Brook wasn't reforming many hearts.

Eagle Brook interpreted the survey results during worship as a summons to be more proactive. Merritt, using visual aids on a giant projection screen, introduced the concept in typically user-friendly fashion by saying that hearts at Eagle Brook need to be expanded "like the Grinch's." A slide showing the Grinch with a growing heart got everybody smiling. With the crowd loosened up, Merritt gently advised members of his flock to adopt five habits in the coming months: regular Bible reading, prayer, solitude, service to the church, and participation in a mentoring relationship. These disciplines help people to look outside themselves and expand their range of concerns. In the months ahead, congregants would have opportunities to learn techniques in each discipline.

Merritt sold the program by apparently anticipating the question natural to his congregation's culture: "How will it help me get what I want?" He was careful to assure his audience that each of these practices would yield a personal payoff. He quoted Psalm 1 and Joshua 1 to assure hearers that the righteous shall "prosper." He showed a video testimony from a woman who had adopted the disciplines and promptly enjoyed better relationships and achieved financial stability. Getting from there to an enhanced spiritual life might be a long road, but perhaps I was witnessing a first step.

Other church leaders were cautious. They knew Merritt was addressing a real need, but they wanted to be sure higher expectations wouldn't diminish Eagle Brook's market share. "The study shows that spiritual growth is what they want," said associate grace pastor Lynne Jeffers after a worship service to kick off the new program. "But if you make it too uncomfortable, they'll go to another church that makes it more comfortable for them."

In rolling out new disciplines, Eagle Brook is trying to challenge its clientele without sparking a backlash, but such an approach is not without risks. Each of Merritt's prescribed practices allows for a great deal of customization. Practitioners can choose, for instance, how they'd like to serve the church or where they'd like to experience solitude. This approach attempts to shape the hearts of churchgoers who don't want their lifestyles cramped, and it isn't guaranteed to succeed. Some may ignore the disciplines altogether. Others may customize them to the point that their concern for others doesn't expand one bit—for instance, if they pray only for their own health and success. Eagle Brook isn't ready to watch its attendees walk out as they routinely do at Woodland Hills. Hence its challenges are far more modest.

Nonetheless, Eagle Brook demonstrates how seeds of challenge can take root even where self-interested spirituality is the norm. Those who try the disciplines and reckon firsthand with biblical themes just might grow to love outcasts in their communities. Hours spent in intentional, silent solitude really *can* help clarify what's important and what's not. It's hard to be involved in mentoring, either as mentor or mentee, without coming to care for the other person and to ponder what it means to progress as a human being. These opportunities therefore create an atmosphere where people can begin practicing self-denial without seeming masochistic or idiotic to their peers. They might even inspire others to follow suit.

Beyond adopting individual disciplines, some members of Eagle Brook are earning special respect from peers and church leaders for being a sacrificial bunch. A small group of nine women stands out as a model in which "God is doing a mighty work," according to groups pastor Sue Lennartson. While most small groups at Eagle Brook disbanded for the summer of 2008, this one—which had already been meeting for an uncommonly long three years—kept meeting weekly to press further into the biblical book of Daniel and to maintain camaraderie. Then, on a fall retreat, group leader Kathleen Woodbury challenged all members to master, with God's help, a nagging area of personal weakness. Several of the women radically changed their diets in bids to lose significant amounts of weight. One resolved to cease a habit of persistent negative thinking. Woodbury herself aimed to cultivate patience by undertaking a twenty-one-day "Daniel Fast," a minimal-intake regimen named for the prophet whose self-denying ways were the subject of the group's fall study. Self-imposed challenges varied, in keeping with the church's individualistic ethic. Even so, these women were gaining respect by coming together in search of something more than comfort. They were actively incurring discomfort in a search for higher rewards, and peers such as Lennartson respected them for it.

To be sure, these personal initiatives weren't the stuff of saints' biographies. Group members uniformly opted for challenges that would deliver personal dividends—their undertakings could not be called selfless. Signs suggested that not everyone had warmed to the idea that spiritual growth may sometimes require hardship. One member, Annie Anderson, said things were going well in her life, but she also feared the prospect of hard times ahead, including her husband's pursuit of a promising but uncertain music career. Hoping to keep personal trials of all types at bay, she asked group members to pray that she would see signs of trouble well in advance "so I don't have to go through a deep valley." Rather than note how God's ways might be more challenging than divine shelter from hardship, her peers simply nodded and offered supportive words. Apparently even in this relatively disciplined small group, people still hope God won't change their hearts by giving them anything other than what they want.

Nevertheless, Eagle Brook's members are in some cases successfully changing their lives by letting others serve as their guides. Woodbury found that her fast, coupled with her group's encouragement to stick with it, bred new habits of gratitude and restraint. She said she was becoming more careful about using a constructive tone with her husband and teenage daughter, and increasingly chose her words with the gracious ways of God in mind.

Similar successes arose from the congregation's three spiritual-direction groups, which used trained directors to help individuals see God at work in their lives. Directors sometimes nudged people to reconsider their plans. For instance, Diane Carlson told her group that she was furious toward her brother for his "extreme" form of disciplining his children. She planned to confront him with righteous indignation. But instead of offering support for whatever she might choose to do, the director and group members refocused her on what it would mean to love her brother. She decided to concentrate on the many good things about him, including many aspects of his parenting. She was glad she did. Within a year, her brother's wife died of cancer. Carlson felt grateful that she had built a foundation of trust for when he needed her. "If I had confronted him, I would have severed the relationship," she said. "I don't think he could have reached out to me after that."

Eagle Brook may not be overflowing with spiritual giants, but its efforts and progress are noteworthy because it is a church that is learning how to read the new religious marketplace. Pastor Merritt is taking baby steps to reframe his church as a spiritual fitness center rather than a religious Cineplex. If he succeeds, then other ambitious churches will surely take note. A new world of possibilities may open up for the market-driven, heart-shaping Church.

Augsburg College, a Minneapolis institution of the mainline Evangelical Lutheran Church in America (ELCA), approaches spiritual formation from a different angle than a parish congregation. But what the school has learned and taught may nonetheless be helpful to many a parish that would like to change its ways yet doesn't know where to begin.

Augsburg lays a foundation for its members by beginning with an assumption: everyone has a vocation, or a calling from above. True to Martin Luther's thinking on the subject, the school regards vocation as encompassing not only one's career but every area of life, including roles in family and church.

Every Augsburg student must pass a two-semester course titled "Christian Vocation and the Search for Meaning." In the course, students try to figure out how their unique gifts can help meet the world's deep needs. A text for the course highlights why individuals should be guided by more than their own wish lists: "In vocation, the individual never stands alone. Rather, the one called is continually acting in the world and responding to the claims of God and the larger community." By emphasizing vocational awareness, Augsburg takes ownership of the Church's eternal mission and asks students to buy in to the project of elevating what matters to them. Securing consent to the heart-shaping process is an auspicious starting point that parishes could easily emulate.

Augsburg brings its heart-shaping techniques to the wider world through travel programs that push students out of their comfort zones. Ordinary churchgoers as well as students from more than three dozen colleges take part annually in international travel seminars through Augsburg's Center for Global Education (CGE). The center structures its two-week trips to Central America and Africa to encourage participants to think and feel in new, unexpected ways.

These programs contrast sharply with those offered by entrepreneurial mission agencies that promise excitement, recreation, and a few days of meaningful work. In Augsburg's programs, students get to know their hosts by spending hours, sometimes days, absorbing the details of their lives and pasts. They don't indulge in the quick gratification of taking control of a construction project and taking pride in day-to-day progress without ever getting to know the beneficiaries. Nor do they try to do a lot of sightseeing, river rafting, or the like. Instead, they defer to their hosts to challenge them in difficult, personal ways and stretch how they perceive people in developing nations. Their process is the harder one because it involves relinquishing control and letting themselves be changed on a deep level. But as the harder pathway, it's also the one that has more impact on the heart.

Host families invite students into their homes and share personal, sometimes wrenching stories. At times, they bring their American guests into workplaces, such as wholesale markets where coffee growers seek prices high enough to feed their families. Seminar participants listen and ask questions as community leaders unpack the significance of what they've seen. They also engage in activities such as finding out how much they can buy in a market with the wages paid to a local, unskilled worker. In combination, the experiences of the CGE's travelers challenge them to reconsider—in light of God's values—what they need to be doing with their lives. When successful, these programs carry out the eternal mission of the Church, albeit in an unconventional form.

When traveling, Augsburg students come face-to-face with human suffering in a way that can make them more compassionate. In El Salvador, for instance, they visit communities where the mentally ill go untreated. In makeshift health clinics, they observe groaning patients whose kidneys failed after they drank contaminated water. With no treatment available, the groaning never ends. Visitors say they can't help but to feel these patients' pain—and to appreciate how they endure.

"People were just suffering," recalled senior Natalie Sasseville. "But people had a joy that we [in America] don't have.... Their life was so much richer than our life." She said what she saw in El Salvador helped her clarify her vocation. She realized: "Our greatest need as Americans is spiritual." She resolved to go into ministry and spend her career battling materialism among American churchgoers.

Other travelers find themselves inspired to take more risks as witness to the Gospel. Senior Joe Skogmo felt he'd encountered for the first time in his life "the essence of Christianity" among Salvadorans. They told him stories about deceased relatives who'd been inspired by Scripture to demand basic human rights from the government and suffered dearly for their courage. He felt compelled to make voluntary sacrifices of his own, perhaps by teaching English under tough conditions in El Salvador. "I'm more open to radical things like that," Skogmo said. "I want to take the Gospel and act upon what it says. [But] look at how they are living out the Gospel in comparison to the way I am. Maybe I need to be more assertive and radicalized."

For Michelle Roulet, a middle-aged student, one humbling experience in San Salvador led to a commitment to be more charitable. She was among the American dinner guests in a proud family's shack made from tin, wood, and other scraps scavenged from around the city. As she watched her puttering hostess, covered in bandages and smiling as she prepared to share from her meager food supply, Roulet felt ashamed.

"My first reaction was, 'How can anyone live this way for longer than a day or two?'" Roulet said. "I felt ashamed of myself for thinking it was so horrible, while they didn't think it was horrible. They were very happy.... I spent the rest of the trip wondering, 'Could I do what these people have done and retain my joy in life?'"

Fearing the honest answer might be "no," Roulet resolved to loosen her attachment to creature comforts by intentionally sharing in others' suffering more often. Doing so would help make their burdens more bearable, she said, and would help her be "joyful despite the circumstances," as Scripture says she should be. Now she keeps an eye out for people, including strangers, who need some kind of assistance. Even if she's busy, she tries to stop what she's doing and be helpful, or somehow share the load. It's not history-changing ministry, she admits, but it is real compassion. And that's no small thing, since it reflects the heart of God.

Augsburg also demonstrates how hearts can grow when people are sent into situations that they find uncomfortable. Religion professor Beverly Stratton, for instance, got to know a very depressed, possibly suicidal student who couldn't seem to find any joy in life. She suggested he travel with CGE to El Salvador, where he'd meet people who had lost their entire families in massacres and would "see hope as you've never seen it before." He wasn't keen on the idea, but she persisted and he went. Though his depression never disappeared, his heavy spirit seemed to lighten through exposure to people who helped put his problems in perspective.

"He wrote amazing poetry about his experience," Stratton remembers. "He sensed the hope in that community ... I think he's experiencing his own life with a little more hope now."

Sometimes bold requirements at Augsburg help open a person's heart to a wider range of cares. That's what happened for Joanna Flaten, a 2008 graduate from Richland, Washington. She originally came to Augsburg with plans to get a degree, return to her upscale hometown, settle down in a nice home with a husband, and maybe have children by her mid-twenties.

Then Augsburg's service-learning requirements brought her into what she admits were sometimes uncomfortable new roles. She tutored children of Somali immigrants, and she volunteered at an overnight homeless shelter. Over time, her goals and passions changed. She came to care deeply about the fragile lives of undocumented immigrants, whom she had come to know, to trust, and to regard as "the most beautiful people." Projects done initially to fulfill requirements morphed into extracurricular ministry as she came to recognize work with immigrants as her vocation.

"What I had expected for my life became almost empty for me," said Flaten, who went on to study for ministry at Luther Seminary. "The community's needs aren't calling me back home."

Students learn the power of challenging others, too. During a youth-ministry internship in Duluth, Augsburg senior Katie Kaiser wasn't sure how to build compassion among teenagers. Drawing on her experience at Augsburg, she gave them an assignment that she hoped would stretch their hearts. Their task was to visit regularly with residents of a low-income retirement community. By design, this ministry setting wasn't one of many choices, since Kaiser knew students wouldn't choose it if offered an easier alternative. All were required to spend time with elders, get to know individuals, plan activities, and reflect with their peers on their experiences. At first, the teens protested that the assignment would be boring or depressing. But they soon built relationships with elders, and their range of cares grew wider. "They weren't opposed to it once they got there,"

Kaiser said. "After that, they were asking to ride in a van that picks up seniors to go to our church. They really came to like and care about older people."

Flaten uses assignments, too, when she works with youth groups. She described the goal as "creating space for grace, because once you become aware of it, it impacts you in a lot of ways." Getting to that goal, she said, involves pushing young people beyond where they want to go. "It may involve creating opportunities to go out in the community and serve in ways that they may not find comfortable and that they may not be used to," Flaten said. "We set it up in advance to explain, 'We're here to meet people, learn from them, and encounter Christ in them.' ... Then after, we ask questions: 'Did you encounter grace there? Just tell me about the people you met.'"

Times of trial are expected in the Augsburg learning environment, but they nevertheless test students' resolve. I visited campus less than two weeks after a student was murdered outside a nearby housing complex, where he had been tutoring schoolchildren through a college work-study program. For twenty-year-old junior Ahmednur Ali, working with children in the Somali immigrant neighborhood of Cedar-Riverside had represented a chance to give back to his own ethnic community. But that mission came to a sudden end on a Monday afternoon in September 2008 when a gunman shot him outside the Bryan Coyle Community Center where he'd been tutoring. Police initially charged another man of Somali descent in the crime but ended up dropping charges due to insufficient evidence.

Three weeks after the deadly incident, Augsburg president Paul Pribbenow gave a sermon urging the grieving community not to "pull back into the safety of our campus and go on about our business." He urged all to remember: "God has called us to be a neighbor here, to do acts of mercy and to make this a place of hospitality and mutual respect." Not all heeded his vision. Katie Kaiser said that many of her classmates who had been considering field-work options in the city chose instead to pursue placements farther away, in seemingly safer suburbs. The murder, she said, had led them to rethink whether an urban ministry would be worth the personal risk.

To be sure, Augsburg, like other institutions, has plenty of room for improvement. Sometimes its trips to developing nations merely reinforce preexisting attitudes and political viewpoints. For instance, three members of Holy Trinity Lutheran Church in Minneapolis told me that their church trip with Augsburg's CGE to Cuba in 2002 had only strengthened their long-held positive opinions about that country's health-care and education systems. Though they found the trip refreshing and re-energizing, none of them could point to a way in which their personal cares or concerns had changed. This suggests that Augsburg's programs sometimes attract people who are seeking a type of comforting affirmation, and the school delivers. The school's community-outreach programs seem to be subject to similar dynamics, with some students taking part in outreach programs that they expect to be comfortable. Perhaps those who continued to serve in urban neighborhoods after the 2008 murder felt they weren't risking danger since the tragic incident may have traced to an internal conflict within the Somali community. It's impossible to know for sure, but it seems safe to say Augsburg hasn't yet figured out how to encourage everyone within its sphere of influence to live and love beyond their comfort zones. This leaves the institution with challenges for the future.

Augsburg has nonetheless tapped an important chord in American religion. The school has learned how to help students and churchgoers hear their callings as new concerns come to replace old ones. For those willing to be changed on the level that matters most to God, the institution has put structures in place to make it happen.

What's happening in a few corners of the Twin Cities suggests that both the Church and the new religious marketplace could have a brighter future ahead. Christians are recognizing their churches have more to offer than spiritually seasoned entertainment or reassuring platitudes. They're showing a degree of spiritual maturity in forgoing certain comforts and prerogatives in order to become the virtuous people that God has called them to be. They're working within a quintessentially American framework of innovation to come up with new models for the age-old, eternally pressing project of shaping hearts. At the same time, they seem to be doing their best to stay true to Scripture and to their spiritual traditions. These developments demonstrate the marketplace's capacity to address religious consumers' deepest needs, the ones that require saying "no" to superficial wants. They tell us that what needs to be done is in fact being done in ordinary American communities.

These stories of church life in Minneapolis/St. Paul by no means represent a new norm. Religious institutions far more frequently serve up the shallower fare that they think helps boost their numbers. What's more, congregations across America will need to wrestle for years to come with a crucial question: how might people in our community go from wanting affirmation to wanting elevation? It will be difficult to even introduce that discussion in many churches, where satisfying desires is understood to be the ticket to growing attendance and revenues. Yet the fact that a handful of churches in Minnesota are pushing people beyond their comfort zones and elevating their personal values means that more could follow suit—and make the Church into the character-shaping force that America desperately needs it to be.

Three core lessons gleaned in the Twin Cities could benefit congregations across America.

First, customers in the religious marketplace are capable of demanding higher quality and getting it. High quality refers not to slick worship services but to systems that effectively elevate hearts. Churchgoers hungry for more than the usual entertain-and-soothe fare are eagerly responding when church institutions make challenging alternatives available. This blunts the argument that churchgoers only flock to congregations that satisfy their wishes or pair them up with people like themselves.

Thus a race to offer grace at the cheapest possible price is not inevitable, even amidst the intense pressures of the religious marketplace.

Second, the church's authentic mission of shaping hearts can and should be carried out in varied forms. What works at Woodland Hills probably wouldn't work at Eagle Brook or Abbey Way, and vice versa. This is an important point, since the American religious landscape is becoming increasingly compartmentalized. It means that churches can push people beyond their comfort zones in productive ways even if those institutions have come to cater to niches based on age, race, political ideology, sexual orientation, or other identity factors. For the church that targets twenty- and thirtysomethings, the appropriate challenge might be for members to spend time visiting, serving, and learning from people fifty years their senior. Liberal and conservative congregations might need structures that compel them to get together over food and swap family stories, since that would make it harder for them to demonize each other. As the Minnesota examples suggest, the tools at the church's disposal are sufficiently varied and adaptable to offer hope for virtually any setting.

Third, heart shaping works best when Christians acknowledge that they need it. People who reached new heights in these congregations were usually willing to take personal risks in order to be transformed by the Gospel. They let themselves forge unlikely connections with people whose circumstances and concerns made a lasting impact on their hearts.

These patterns offer guidance for the tens of millions who support and shape America's Protestant churches. If churchgoers were to do one thing to address the spiritual crisis facing America, it should be to let themselves be changed by the unlikely relationships that flow from following Jesus. No other action could do more to release the heart-shaping power of the Church. The experience of a few Minnesotans points to the extraordinary possibilities.

EPILOGUE

Fixing the Imminent Future

OVER THE NEXT FIFTY YEARS, CHURCH LIFE IN AMERICA will likely change more dramatically than ever before in the nation's history—and in unpredictable ways. The forces of religious consumerism that have been unleashed in recent years are now free to take the Church in directions unimaginable just a generation ago. Everything is in flux: even the common understanding of a church as a community bound by shared Christian beliefs and practices cannot be presumed to apply in the years ahead. In the new religious marketplace, shared preferences for whatever a "church" is offering will be all that holds some religious communities together.

On this wide-open frontier, coming generations will determine which elements endure or get reinvented and which disappear altogether from the Church. What happens to the institution in the next fifty years will determine how American characters are shaped (or not shaped) for centuries. To prepare for the days ahead, Christians need to consider what might unfold if current trends continue or if religious consumers instead put new dynamics into motion.

Considering the contemporary Church's trajectory toward a market-driven version of faith, it is reasonable to expect that in the future churches will increasingly derive as much of their revenue as possible from corporate sponsors. The pattern is already taking root in congregations old and new alike. Across New England, historic churches garner thousands of dollars in yearly rent from cellular-phone companies that hide their towers inside picturesque steeples. This practice keeps ugly towers out of sight in quaint towns, while thrifty churchgoers love the fact that somebody else—say, Verizon Wireless or Sprint—effectively pays a chunk of their ministers' salaries and benefits.

Churches also pad their incomes by selling advertising space in their newsletters. This trend is poised to explode as marketers increasingly value opportunities to reach desirable demographic groups and align themselves with respected organizations. The captive audience that churches offer to potential sponsors is hard to beat. Church attendees increasingly are members of target markets, have disposable income, and favor those who support their faith communities. I expect we'll soon see corporate sponsors on church web sites and banner advertising in large churches, if it hasn't already begun. Even church-naming rights might soon be for sale, if churches follow the lead of stadiums and even a handful of small towns. Such developments in the Church might seem preposterous, but that's what people thought about the idea of church marketing forty years ago. As long as churchgoers want to get more for less, church leaders will keep presenting new types of corporate partnerships as win-win opportunities. Corporate sponsorships could be the key to divorcing sacrifice from faith once and for all.

At the same time, the landscape of niche religious experiences will likely grow more varied and specialized than ever before. New churches or small groups may, for example, cater to unmarried blue-collar workers, retired professional couples, or young outdoorsy families with kids. If affinity groups successfully attract attendees, then highly specialized groups will be especially attractive.

Just about any type of "church" can emerge in this environment. The current "emerging church" movement, which emphasizes creativity over doctrine, is laying groundwork for a new generation of independent start-up churches with no uniform standards for beliefs or behavior. In this milieu, the bizarre and extreme may take root alongside the mainstream. Groups organized to advance ideologies, such as the notoriously white supremacist World Church of the Creator, used to be roundly dismissed for betraying true church principles. But such sweeping condemnation for misuse of the term *church* becomes harder to sustain when there's no widespread agreement about what those principles should be.

While today's niche churches are still curiosities, tomorrow's will be commonplace as congregations learn to purge all influences that might offend. Church as an institution that ideally transcends boundaries of class and race will be an increasingly antiquated concept in this landscape of self-selecting niches, where worshippers log onto the Internet to pray virtually alongside people who share their viewpoints—wherever they may be—and never hear the prayers of next-door neighbors who see the world a little bit differently.

This future Church, stripped of challenging forces and freighted with inertia, would bode ill for character formation across American society. Signs already suggest that values long associated with the Church are disturbingly scarce in American culture. Redemption, for instance, doesn't seem to count for much in a society that routinely tears down leaders by exposing their past affiliations or lapses in judgment. The Church would have us act differently: since everyone is sinful, those who openly admit mistakes and make amends should be appreciated for their candor and humility. But too often the press and public seem to regard this messy, restorative process of redemption as a kiss of death for any would-be leader. Apparently the semblance of perfection in a leader, however false, is what Americans prefer to see.

Similarly, prisoners on death row experience little evidence that their society takes seriously the Christian teaching that no one is beyond hope. Modeling God's concern for rehabilitating sinners doesn't seem to be a priority for American lawmakers or their constituents, especially in states with big Protestant majorities. While redeeming fallen souls may be a Christian value, it's a well-repressed one in a society where a more primitive, vengeful sense of justice often triumphs.

Other Christian values seem to be eroding in American culture in this era of nominal church influence. Declining civility in public discourse, as witnessed in settings from the blogosphere to Capitol Hill, suggests that few care to extend respect to all as a sign of God's universal love for humankind.

Compassion, too, seems to be waning as Americans bristle at the notion that they should suffer with those in need. Fundraisers increasingly try to make philanthropy as fun and painless as possible, offering everything from gala events to credit cards that painlessly steer a percentage of sale proceeds to a card user's favorite cause. Americans may still want to help their neighbors with a donation (as long as they get a tax deduction), but they certainly don't want to suffer with them, as witnessed in many a festive fundraiser, charity golf tournament, and gated community.

Redemption, civility, and compassion enjoy honored status in the Christian tradition because they reflect values associated with God in Scripture. But they're in short supply as the customer-driven Church fails to instill them in its people. These values will continue to fade if current trends lead to their logical end, that is, to a Church with no muscle to expand members' capacities for personal sacrifice and humility. But such a future is not a foregone conclusion.

Religious consumers could steer the Church to build a foundation for shaping character and values well into the twenty-second century. In years ahead, churchgoers could decide they don't need religion to be spiritual comfort food—they need a spiritual gymnasium, to get their souls in shape. Gyms come in many different forms, but they all aim to deliver physical fitness by offering their clientele appropriate challenges. Similarly, churches might build new programs and reinvigorate sacred practices with an eye toward fostering virtue among their customers. They might playfully facilitate lunches between feuding parties to resolve conflicts before Communion is served. Parishioners might request certain types of challenges, such as meditative prayer sessions for chronic multitaskers, as they become more aware of what a well-toned spiritual body looks like. Children might learn in age-appropriate lessons how their desires reflect commercial messages delivered via television and other media. Teachers might coach them in how to develop cravings for higher things. In these and other ways, churches could tap the resources they already have in their communities to meet an increasingly acute need for character shaping.

On the organizational level, the Church in coming decades could intentionally push back against problems generated by the new religious marketplace. Churches might actively resist, for instance, when corporations offer to underwrite ministries. In so doing they would be maintaining the tradition of sacrifice as faithful response.

When churches see corporations dangling freebies in front of them, they could recognize the situation for what it is: a challenge to be more resourceful and to be satisfied with less.

They might decline to partner with retailers who'd like to give away free back-to-school supplies as part of a church's outreach ministry. By doing so, they'd resist making discipleship ever more cost-free, which is what happens when Christians let deep-pocketed organizations underwrite their charitable giving. They'd also preserve their integrity: churches shouldn't have to worry about offending sponsors when they denounce how corporations deliberately inflame and manipulate Americans' most primitive desires. Such a shift away from accepting sponsorships wouldn't come at anyone else's expense. Needy kids wouldn't have to go without supplies, since retailers could distribute goods through a nonprofit agency. Yet churches would benefit spiritually. By choosing to give away only what they can generate through internal donations, churches would be taking a step to recover the virtue-shaping connection between generosity and personal sacrifice. The act of saying "no, thank you" would in itself build character.

Churches might go even further by exploring new ways to elevate desires. Just as they now compare notes on what works to boost worship attendance, they might in the future share best practices for broadening what churchgoers deeply care about. Pastors could receive specialized training in how to apply insights from cutting-edge brain science to counseling, preaching, or other areas of ministry. Laypeople could examine whether they're coddling themselves by associating mostly with like-minded people in church. They could analyze what needs to change for them to encounter more Christians who will challenge them.

Congregations could also draw from existing traditions to improve their ability to build character in spite of the new religious marketplace. A tradition like storytelling at Christmas could be augmented by encouraging parishioners of all ages to talk about times in their lives when a self-centered desire gave way to a holy one. A new tradition would likely take shape as churchgoers consider, through these shared anecdotes, how desires get reformed and why the process is so important. Such institutional frameworks could become enduring, dynamic features of the American religious landscape if they're planted and solidified during the upcoming decades.

The effect of the next few years of American Christianity will reverberate far beyond the institution itself. At stake for rising generations of Christians is nothing less than their understanding of what Christianity is all about. Perhaps they'll come to understand it as one of my parishioners did; she hoped her teenage son "would see God as a resource" to help him realize all his dreams. Or perhaps they'll see themselves more as people with a calling from God than as people who imagine God to be at their beck and call. Either attitude would influence which factors they consider when deciding what to do with their lives or how to assess what matters most from one day to the next. The ultimate concerns of tomorrow's Christians hang in the balance.

How the Church evolves will affect every realm of American life. That's because individuals reared in and shaped by churches bring their moral values to bear in settings from town-council chambers to corporate boardrooms, from office cubicles to the stands at youth hockey games. Those molded to reflect a God who honors every soul, for instance, would more likely deal honestly with coworkers than spread rumors to squelch perceived competition. Since few other institutions in America make a point to inculcate lofty moral values, the Church bears primary responsibility for making sure its people bring concerns for justice, mercy, and other noble values into the public square. Whether public discourse includes respectful arguments for defending the weak or redeeming the guilty will depend largely on how well the Church transmits such values in the years ahead.

Americans would be remiss to assume that whatever emerges from the religious marketplace in years ahead will be benign. Religion's unfortunate capacity for destructiveness is unleashed when the Church abdicates its core mission. For instance, churches became apologists for slavery in the nineteenth century when they lost sight of their mandate to bear witness for social equality. The Southern Presbyterian Church went so far as to declare in 1864: "it is the peculiar mission of the Southern Church to conserve the institution of slavery." At other stressful times in history, wayward churches have come to sanction such sins as apartheid and anti-Semitism. In these cases and others, political ideology and/or nationalistic fervor have hijacked weak churches that failed to stay focused on their mission. Today, since market forces aren't always conscientious, the Church is even more vulnerable to exploitation for unworthy or evil causes. Many a dangerous initiative would love to enlist religious zeal on its side. To regard market-driven religion as necessarily innocuous is to help prepare the way for disaster.

On the global stage, major crises of the twenty-first century already demand that Americans develop the fortitude to make personal sacrifices for the common good. A number of public crises have demonstrated that the American soul is already undergoing a profound crisis of character. The financial crisis of 2008 left the world wishing Americans hadn't been so quick to profit at others' expense by lending to unqualified borrowers and trafficking toxic assets across borders in tidy packages. Painfully absent were habits of self-restraint and self-denial at times when intense temptations called for strong character.

As energy-policy debates rage, an underlying issue is whether Americans' personal desires can be reformed and elevated. Countries concerned about global warming hope for a day when Americans can restrain their appetites for unnecessarily big vehicles, big homes, and inexpensive fossil fuels. As it is, our world's fate may be dictated by a collective surrender to gluttony.

Even international security issues shine a spotlight on American character. When Americans torture suspected terrorists and disregard habeas corpus in a quest to feel safer, the world rightly wonders whether Americans possess sufficient moral strength to choose what's right over what's expedient. Though many factors have contributed to this character deficit, the Church's failure to elevate souls in its immediate sphere of influence surely hasn't helped. If the Church can recover and exercise its elevating power in the coming decades, then it will be doing its part to help America bless the world by practicing honorable, disciplined habits of the heart.

The Church has everything it needs to become a formidable force for good in American society. Social networks, meeting spaces, and institutions of higher learning are just a few of the abundant resources waiting to be redeployed in the recovery of the institution's God-given mission. Christianity's rich spiritual tradition stands ready to guide and inspire in a time when character shaping is widely needed. But this tradition will surely become more foreign and less accessible to future generations if today's consumers opt to let it languish.

To meet the present challenge, people on all levels should take steps to build the Church's heart-shaping muscles. Laypeople need to challenge one another to move beyond their comfort zones, love the seemingly unlovable, and practice self-denial for the sake of cultivating virtue. They need to call on every ministry in their lives to help them and their peers to display—unmistakably and with greater fullness over time—the gifts of the Spirit (Galatians 5:22) and the character of Jesus Christ. Clergy need to lead by example. They should use every resource at their disposal to encourage a church culture that values difficult challenge on the level of the heart. They'd do well to view themselves less as consolers or performers on a stage for God and more as trainers who set high standards and help people master their desires through grace and habit. Even people uninvolved in church life have a constructive role to play. Everyone who cares about character formation in America should encourage intrepid Christians as they strive to reclaim and reinterpret their tradition's long-neglected ascetic roots. Instead of ridiculing those who temper their appetites, observers should appreciate them as fledgling antidotes to a culture prone to greed and despair. In present-day America, these Christian mavericks will have to contend with countless distractions, pressures, and temptations to abdicate their higher callings. But they'll have a better chance of succeeding if they get support from a range of individuals who think character still matters.

Few moments in history have offered ordinary people so much opportunity to shape the institution that points to the highest things. Getting it right will be worth the effort.

ACKNOWLEDGMENTS

I wasn't the only one who believed years ago that this book needed to be written. Nor was I alone in making sacrifices to bring it into existence. Many people shaped the ideas in these pages through generous gifts of curiosity, attention, prayer, skepticism and critique. I'm in debt to more than can be acknowledged here, but a few were so significant that I'd be remiss not to mention them by name.

My editor at Basic Books, Lara Heimert, showed confidence in my thesis from the first time we discussed it over eggs and coffee in 2006. Just as importantly, she believed in my then-unproven ability to execute a project of this scope. Her vision helped this book find its proper form, and her edits put me on a strict word diet that I'm sure will be good for my heart in the long run. To her craftsmanship and work ethic, I tip my hat.

Brandon Proia, former associate editor at Basic, made the manuscript stronger by exercising his knack for knowing when an idea is incomplete—or overdone—and exactly what's needed to fix a writer's self-made entanglements. He challenged me on all levels, from renderings of history to semantic subtleties, and left this book much better than he found it.

This text never would have reached the cutting room floor at Basic were it not for the hard work and insight of my agent and fellow Newburyporter, Lisa Adams of the Garamond Agency. For more than a year, she patiently reviewed drafts of my proposal and guided the process of getting it ready for prime-time. She's been helpful at every stage, which makes her a gem in her field.

Long before the professionals got involved in this project, I fed on the inspirational wisdom and encouragement of friends and family. Bob Gould, father of my late and much-missed brother-in-law Rob Gould, has been telling me since the mid-1990s at annual holiday gatherings: "I know you have a book in you. When are you going to write it?" I thought back to his unwavering confidence at many a frustrating juncture in the writing process. I'm looking forward to Thanksgiving.

Eric Wybenga, a gifted writer and loyal friend, listened to me on wooded trails by the Merrimack River, in New York restaurants and anywhere else where I could track him down. His sense that these ideas, once cleaned up, might actually be book-worthy convinced me to embark on this journey.

Along the way, I've had a few providential breaks. One involved having a grad school friend and canoeing buddy, Frederick Simmons, who just happens to be a world-class theological ethicist at Yale. On gorgeous days spent paddling Western New England's rivers, he indulged me time and again with opportunities to talk through my latest thoughts on sanctification and grace. Then we'd find a muddy spot to eat lunch and talk sports or politics before notching another 10 or 15 miles in the canoe. Providence indeed.

Another involved a great mentor. John H. "Jack" Adams gave me my first journalism job at the *Goldsboro News-Argus* in North Carolina. He taught me how to talk slow, write fast, laugh a lot and make a living as a writer. Lessons learned in his shop, plus his unflagging enthusiasm and confidence in my abilities, set me up to do OK in this business. I'm forever in his debt.

My research in Minnesota benefitted greatly from a few people who helped me track down great sources and schedule time with them. Tonya Toutge of Abbey Way smoothed my way to spend a lot of informative time with her fellow congregants. Ann Butwell of Augsburg College fielded many e-mails and calls from me and arranged highly productive meetings for me on the Augsburg campus. Others helped me make fruitful connections in Minnesota including Sue Lennartson at Eagle Brook and Sandra Unger at Woodland Hills. I'm grateful for all their help.

Family members have been consistently interested and supportive. My sister, Bonnie MacDonald, and her husband Tim Thomas talked with me at length about the problems and possibilities that they and I see in the American church. My nieces, Olivia and Louisa Gould, cheered me on with requests for frequent progress reports. My parents, Lois and George MacDonald, to whom this book is dedicated, gave me everything from faith, hope and love to work habits and a fine education. Each of those gifts shaped this book profoundly. I can't thank my parents enough.

Providence continues. I thank the two boys in my life, Robbie and Ryan Hayes, for letting me play a role in their upbringing and for bearing with me and my moods during this sometimes-trying process. And I'm grateful to my sweetheart, Debora Hayes, who gave up a lot—including many weekend outings and other time together—in order to make this book a reality. She brings beauty, strength and love into my life each day. She knows the Source of all our blessings—even the ones that make life hard sometimes. For that and for her, I give thanks.

NOTES

INTRODUCTION

xi **"In 1955, only 4 percent"**: Robert Wuthnow, *The Restructuring of American Religion* (Princeton University Press, 1988), p. 88.

xi **"…a whopping 44 percent"**: Pew Forum on Religion & Public Life, "U.S. Religious Landscape Survey" (2008), p. 5. This survey, with a sample size of 35,000, ranks among the most comprehensive surveys of American religious life ever conducted.

xi **"Among Protestants"**: Pew Forum on Religion & Public Life, "Faith in Flux: Changes in Religious Affiliation in the U.S." (2009), pp. 5–6.

xii **"Americans find options galore"**: Diana L. Eck, *A New Religious America: How a "Christian Country" Has Become the World's Most Religiously Diverse Nation* (HarperOne, 2001), pp. 3-4.

xvi **"…with more than 100 million adherents:** For a detailed breakdown of Protestant identities in America, see data tables on pp. 4–5 of the American Religious Identification Survey (Trinity College, 2009).

CHAPTER ONE

5 **"'God knows where the money is'"**: Laurie Goodstein, "Believers Invest in the Gospel of Getting Rich," *The New York Times,* August 16, 2009.

7 **"Desert fathers and mothers"**: Laurie Guy, *Introducing Early Christianity: A Topical Survey of Its Life, Beliefs & Practices* (Inter-Varsity Press, 2004), p. 140.

10 **"Members broke off to form new churches"**: The church I pastored in Amesbury, Massachusetts, was the product of one such schism in the early 1830s.

10 **"Shakers established communes"**: Jenkins, Philip. *A History of the United States, Second Edition,* (Palgrave Macmillan, 1997), p. 109.

10 **"Activits for womens' rights"**: Hoffert, Sylvia D. *When Hens Crow: The Woman's Rights Movement in Antebellum America,* (Indiana University Press, 1995), p. 58.

11 **"Methodists drew followers"**: Roger Finke and Rodney Stark, *The Churching of America, 1776–1990* (Rutgers University Press, 1992), p. 85.

12 **"naturally formed planet"**: Sydney E. Ahlstrom, *A Religious History of the American People* (Yale University Press, 1972), pp. 766–767.

12 **"'We want no heaven.'"**: Tim Dowley, ed., *Eerdmans' Handbook to Christianity in America* (William B. Eerdmans, 1983), pp. 300–301.

13 **"Ernest Dichter, an influential expert"**: David Halberstam, *The Fifties* (Villard, 1993), pp. 506–507.

14 **"Sunday-school attendance figures blossomed"**: Dowley, *Eerdmans' Handbook to Christianity in America,* p. 430.

14 **"New attendees had practical, often civic, reasons"**: Robert Wuthnow, After Heaven: Spirituality in America Since the 1950s (University of California Press, 1998), pp. 27–30.

14 **"Congressman Joseph McCarthy's anti-Communist purge"**: Ahlstrom, *A Religious History of the American People,* pp. 951–952.

14 **"a full 75 percent of Americans"**: Wuthnow, *After Heaven,* p. 30.

14 **"the modern American landscape"**: Edwin Gaustad and Leigh Schmidt, *The Religious History of America: The Heart of the American Story from Colonial Times to Today* (HarperSanFrancisco, 2002), p. 342.

14 **"Clergy sought a serene ambience"**: Wuthnow, *After Heaven*, p. 30.

15 **"Christians were bound to have disagreements"**: Wuthnow, *The Restructuring of American Religion* (Princeton University Press, 1988), pp. 68–69.

15 **"Political activism, a familiar feature of church life"**: Ibid., pp. 64–67.

16 **"Skeptics saw the institution as part of the cultural establishment"**: Ahlstrom, *A Religious History of the American People*, p. 1085. Author's note: African American churches, as hubs of political activism in the civil-rights movement, marked an exception to this overall trend.

16 **"Disillusioned clerics"**: Hugh McLeod, *The Religious Crisis of the 1960s* (Oxford University Press, 2008), pp. 190–194. McLeod notes that the exodus of clergy was especially dramatic in Roman Catholicism, where many priests had come to resent celibacy requirements as well as their declining social status. He adds that Protestant clergy, though not required to be celibate, nonetheless shared many of the pressures and frustrations of their Catholic colleagues. Author's note: as the Vietnam War entered its later years, students increasingly avoided military service by enrolling in seminaries, which eventually boosted the ranks of clergy again. Those years also brought a revival of interest in ministry as idealists envisioned the church as a potential force for social change.

16 **"Americans also sought spiritual enlightenment beyond conventional religion"**: Ahlstrom, *A Religious History of the American People*, pp. 1050–1054.

17 **"a life of faith would hereafter"**: Wuthnow in *After Heaven* regards the journey motif as the overarching concept for American spirituality in and after the 1960s.

17 **"The Episcopal Church began permitting its members in 1968"**: Wuthnow, *The Restructuring of American Religion*, p. 92.

19 **"the Society of Separationists formed in 1963"**: Ibid., pp. 115, 110.

19 **"parachurch groups grew more than 30 percent"**: Ibid., p. 113.

20 **"Even those who hungered"**: As Wuthnow observes on page 93 in *After Heaven*: "Discipline came quickly to reflect the life-styles that matched Americans' personal interests."

25 **"This process allows for virtue"**: Saint Augustine, translated by Anna S. Benjamin and L.H. Hackstaff, *On Free Choice of the Will* (Prentice Hall, 1964), p. 34.

25 **"'our will, principally because of its corruption'"**: John Dillenberger, ed., *Martin Luther: Selections from His Writings* (Doubleday, 1962), pp. 182, 203.

26 **"As early as the 1950s"**: Halberstam, *The Fifties*, p. 226.

27 **"requires substantial personal cost"**: Wuthnow, *After Heaven*, p. 112.

27 **"giving about $100 billion"**: "Giving USA 2008," a report of the Giving USA Foundation.

CHAPTER TWO

34 **"He said that staging Halo games"**: Matt Richtel, "Thou Shalt Not Kill, Except in a Popular Video Game at Church," *The New York Times,* October 7, 2007.

36 **"By 2008, the percentage had reached 65"**: "New Research Describes Use of Technology in Churches," The Barna Group, April 28, 2008.

36 **"more than 180 churches in 2008"**: Ashley Gipson, "Cinema Churches Bring God to the Big Screen—and to Where the People Are," Religion News Service, 2008.

37 **"every time a church spends $15,000"**: Partners in Development, a nonprofit group, works with churches and individuals to build homes in Haiti at $3,000 a piece. See www.pidonline.org.

37 **"Stine makes his living"**: Brad Stine, *Live from Middle America: Rants from a Red-State Comedian* (Hudson Street Press, 2006), pp. 15–20.

37 **"the liberal himself, is God"**: Ibid., p. 111.

39 **"lyrics in jazz"**: Congregational singing isn't entirely absent from all jazz worship services. Some Sunday morning jazz services let congregants sing a few old-time hymns, for instance, with a sort of jazz accompaniment. This marks an improvement upon services where attendees just listen and never sing. But worship dynamics are still disturbingly passive when most of the singing in a jazz service is done by a soloist or choir, or when jazz instrumentals substitute for sermons, which are common practices.

42 **"Why would you rob"**: This comment came from John Hughes, pastor of First Parish Church Congregational in Manchester-by-the-Sea, Massachusetts, when I interviewed him for a story on offering trends.

42 **"Another insisted that the service include no prayers"**: Even though the groom was an atheist, the bride wanted the trappings of a nice church wedding, so he agreed to go along with the program as long as they could find a minister who would, for a fee, purge all references to God. I declined, but they quickly found another minister who was willing.

44 **"sign and symbol of God's grace"**: Protestantism encompasses a range of theological understandings of baptism. Some African American churches, for instance, emphasize baptism as a saving

rite. Old New England traditions tend to view it more as a symbol than as an actual soul-saving experience. But despite this diversity of understandings, it's universally accepted as a sacrament, which at a minimum means an emblem of God's saving grace.

46 **"I was trying to restore appreciation"**: In the early centuries of Christianity, postulants seeking baptism spent three years preparing. The process involved oversight in the disciplined life, self-examination, and periods of fasting before being baptized on Easter morning—a sign of dying and rising with Christ.

48 **"That would sometimes mean comforting the afflicted"**: These phrases describing the highest purpose of the newspaper, attributed to turn-of-the-century journalist Finley Peter Dunne, are often invoked in preaching classes to describe some of the purposes of the sermon.

49 **"At least one preaching expert"**: James Webb, dean of communications at Palm Beach Atlantic University, told me in a 2004 interview: "It is going to be impossible to preach without using humor. You will not be able to stand up and hold the people if you cannot work the stage."

50 **"Though cultural-sensitivity training remains"**: David A. Livermore, *Serving with Eyes Wide Open: Doing Short-Term Missions with Cultural Intelligence* (Baker, 2006), p. 115.

51 **"A whopping 1.6 million people"**: Robert Wuthnow, a sociologist of religion at Princeton University, provided this data, based on his own survey research, for my June 2006 story in *USA Today* titled "On a Mission—A Short-term Mission."

52 **"Payments from mission agencies"**: David A. Livermore, author of *Serving with Eyes Wide Open: Doing Short-Term Missions with Cultural Intelligence*, told me in an interview: "Often there's too high a price for them to say no to this because often [hosting a group] is the means to getting the check that will help support them."

54 "'several awesome worship services'": *The Eagle*, newsletter of Portsmouth Christian Academy, spring 2008, p. 4.

CHAPTER THREE

64 "'It pleased you to transform'": Augustine of Hippo (aka Saint Augustine), *Confessions* (Penguin Classics, 1961), p. 144.

64 "one in every five Americans": Robert Wuthnow, ed., *I Come Away Stronger: How Small Groups Are Shaping American Religion* (Wm. B. Eerdmans, 1994), p. 373.

65 "They say nary a word": Ibid., p. 356.

65 "even among religious conservatives": Ibid., p. 360.

65 "but this rarely happened": Greg L. Hawkins and Cally Parkinson, *Reveal: Where Are You?* (Willow Creek, 2007), pp. 4, 100.

66 "to keep people involved with the institution": Bill Bishop, *The Big Sort: Why the Clustering of Like-Minded America Is Tearing Us Apart* (Houghton Mifflin, 2008), pp. 159–181. This chapter on religion provides an excellent discussion of a much-replicated strategy to grow churches by giving people of similar backgrounds and attitudes a place to connect.

66 "'the church was not helping me'": LifeWay Research, 2006 report on the formerly churched.

68 "In colonial days": E. Brooks Holifield, *A History of Pastoral Care in America: From Salvation to Self-Realization* (Abingdon Press, 1983), p. 47.

68 "Pastors-in-training studied": Samuel T. Armstrong, *The Young Minister's Companion* (Boston, 1813). Baxter's "The Reformed Pastor" is included in this volume, which Armstrong circulated as a popular resource for pastors and seminarians of his day.

68 "By the late nineteenth century": Holifield, *A History of Pastoral Care in America*, p. 176.

79 **"In 2006, 34 percent":** Cremation Association of North America website: http://www.cremationassociation.org/html/about.html
81 **"Americans of all political stripes":** Bishop, *The Big Sort*, pp. 12–13.

CHAPTER FOUR

89 **"63 percent approved of the use of torture":** Pew Forum on Religion & Public Life, "The Religious Dimensions of the Torture Debate," April 29, 2009: http://pewforum.org/docs/?DocID=156.
90 **"Respondents who said":** According to Pew's April 2009 torture survey, 74 percent of those who said they attend services at least a few times a year approved of torture. Among those who seldom or never attend, 69 percent said torture could be justified.
90 **"the more one goes to church":** I first saw this formulation of the survey's meaning in an open letter to Jesus penned by Mercer University ethicist David Gushee and published through Associated Baptist Press on May 5, 2009.
90 **"Left-leaning religious leaders":** Greg Warner, "Evangelicals Seem Unfazed by Torture. Why?" Religion News Service, May 6, 2009.
91 **"By 2007, the count had reached 1,250":** Scott Thumma and Dave Travis, *Beyond Megachurch Myths* (Jossey-Bass, 2007), pp. 6,7.
93 **"Meanwhile, fewer than one in 100":** Kenneth Ferraro, director of the Purdue University Center on Aging and the Life Course, reported these findings in the June 2006 issue of *The Journal for the Scientific Study of Religion.*
93 **"about 75 percent of clerics":** Results of a 2001 national survey of 2,500 religious leaders conducted by Pulpit & Pew, a Duke Divinity School research project: http://www.pulpitandpew.duke.edu/clergyhealth.html.

93　**"overweight and otherwise unhealthy clergy"**: Daniel Burke, "Churches Feel the Pinch of Rising Health Care Costs," Religion News Service, 2008.

93　**"the root of dignity"**: This commentary on the root of dignity is widely attributed to twentieth-century Jewish theologian Abraham Joshua Heschel.

96　**"More than seven out of every ten"**: Josephson Institute, "Report Card on the Ethics of American Youth," 2002.

97　**"Congregants grew more concerned"**: This trend stirred Princeton University sociologist of religion Robert Wuthnow to conclude: "It is unfortunate ... if churches no longer influence how people think concerning bribes and other matters of financial ethics." Robert Wuthnow, *After the Baby Boomers: How Twenty- and Thirty-Somethings Are Shaping the Future of American Religion* (Princeton University Press, 2007), pp. 145–148.

97　**"One magazine for pastors"**: *Leadership Journal* survey, conducted in 2001.

98　**"But even Barna's critics"**: Rice University sociologist D. Michael Lindsay argues that Christians have a better-than-average track record with marriage in "Three Myths About Christians and Divorce" in the March/April 2009 edition of *Rev!* magazine. He says churchgoing evangelicals divorce far less often (the divorce rate in this population is 34 percent) than evangelicals who attend church infrequently (54 percent). One possible explanation could be that, to avoid gossip and shame, evangelicals stop going to church when their marriages get strained beyond repair.

98　**"As Barna Group founder George Barna"**: Barna writes in his 1999 report that the research "raises questions regarding the effectiveness of how churches minister to families. The ultimate responsibility for a marriage belongs to the husband and wife, but the high incidence of divorce within the Christian community challenges the idea that churches provide truly practical and life-changing support for marriages." See "Christians are more likely to experience divorce than are non-Christians," Barna Research Group, Dec. 21, 1999.

100 **"In a 2006 survey"**: LifeWay Research, report on "church switchers," based on a survey of 415 respondents in December 2006.

100 **"conflict in the Church"**: Mark Chaves, "How Common Is Congregational Conflict?" February 25, 2009, *Duke Divinity Call & Response Blog*, www.faithandleadership.com/blog.

101 **"Branding has become a focal project"**: For example, public-relations officers for a range of denominations made branding their focus when they met in Boston in March 2009 for the national convention of the Religion Communicators Council.

106 **"A person can go through"**: According to megachurch experts Scott Thumma and Dave Travis, in megachurches, "each individual and family can create their own custom experience of the congregation. They can participate in this place on their own terms." Thumma and Travis, *Beyond Megachurch Myths*, p. 50.

108 **"churches with slick marketing"**: Theologian Philip Kenneson, coauthor of *Selling Out the Church: The Dangers of Church Marketing* (Wipf & Stock, 1997), helped make me aware of this issue when I interviewed him for a story.

108 **"In 1990, 86 percent of all Americans"**: American Religious Identification Survey 2008. Conducted by Trinity College's Institute for the Study of Secularism in Society. Principal investigators are Barry A. Kosmin and Ariela Keysar.

109 **"just 10 percent of Americans"**: David T. Olson, *The American Church in Crisis* (Zondervan, 2008), pp. 16, 29.

110 **"'Without satisfied customers'"**: Norman Shawchuck, Philip Kotler, Bruce Wrenn, and Gustave Rath. *Marketing to Congrega-*

tions: Choosing to Serve People More Effectively (Nashville: Abingdon Press, 1992), p. 62.

110 **"Executive pastors"**: Seth Godin, *Purple Cow: Transform Your Business by Being Remarkable* (Portfolio, 2003).

110 **"cite Seth Godin's book"**: Jeannie Choi, now assistant editor at *Sojourners* magazine, said she made this discovery when she worked at *Outreach* magazine and interviewed several of the pastors whose congregations topped the Outreach 100 list.

111 **"'How do you connect'"**: Douglas B. Sosnik, Matthew J. Dowd, and Ron Fournier, *Applebee's America: How Successful Political, Business, and Religious Leaders Connect with the New American Community* (Simon & Schuster, 2006), p. 2.

111 **"weeds out 'free riders'"**: Laurence Iannaccone, "Why Strict Churches Are Strong," *The American Journal of Sociology,* vol. 99 (March 1994), pp. 1180–1210.

111 **"Megachurch participants are indeed more likely"**: Thumma and Travis, *Beyond Megachurch Myths*, p. 101.

113 **"Research suggests that such behaviors"**: Iannaccone, "Why Strict Churches Are Strong," p. 1205.

113 **"A full 71 percent"**: National survey by Pew Forum on Religion & Public Life and Pew Research Center for the People & the Press, published August 24, 2006, p. 7. See http://pewforum .org/publications/surveys/religion-politics-06.pdf

CHAPTER FIVE

118 **"They fear that 'the pervasiveness'"**: Philip D. Kenneson and James L. Street, *Selling Out the Church: The Dangers of Church Marketing* (Cascade Books, originally through Abingdon Press, 1997), p. 52.

118 **"Megachurches have grown exponentially"**: Thumma and Travis, *Beyond Megachurch Myths*, pp. 15–17.

120 **"they've been disenfranchised"**: A 2006 LifeWay Research survey of 415 Protestants who had switched churches found that 18 percent believed people at their former church were "judgmental of others." Another 14 percent said their former church "didn't seem to be a place where God was at work." Together, these findings suggest that one in three respondents had experienced personal hurt in the church to such a degree that they left the community forever.

122 **"Up until the late third century"**: Priests in Catholicism and Anglicanism would later trace their clerical authority to Peter, whom Jesus identified as the rock of the church (Matthew 16:18). But the establishment of clergy as a particular class of Christian with special duties wouldn't come to pass until the third century.

122 **"As late as 200 A.D.,"**: Stephen Charles Neill and Hans Ruedi Weber, eds., *The Layman in Christian History* (Westminster Press, 1963), pp. 31–32.

123 **"Cyprian, bishop of Carthage"**: Ibid., p. 36.

123 **"In practice, this meant"**: Ibid., p. 36

124 **"feel unchallenged and disappointed"**: LifeWay's 2006 survey of people who had changed churches found that the most common reason people move from one church to another is that the "church was not helping me to develop spiritually." This suggests, among other things, a hunger for more-meaningful church experiences. Conscientious religious consumerism may help satisfy that hunger.

125 **"They could rest assured that"**: John Dillenberger, ed., *Martin Luther: Selections from His Writings* (Anchor/Doubleday, 1962), p. 349. The Luther quote is from his essay, "The Pagan Servitude of the Church."

125 **"They would sometimes fast and pray"**: David D. Hall, *Worlds of Wonder, Days of Judgment: Popular Religious Belief in Early New England,* (Harvard University Press, 1989), p. 170.

126 **"Women-led humanitarian organizations"**: Tomczak, Patricia. "Women and Religion in America, 1600-1900," at http://www .alliancelibrarysystem.com/IllinoisWomen/rel.htm

127 **"In 2005, consumers internationally spent"**: Fairtrade Labelling Organizations International: www.fairtrade.net.

128 **"congregations in at least eight Protestant denominations"**: For a list of denominations with Fair Trade initiatives, see https:// www.pcusa.org/trade/links.htm

134 **"Over time, they become more aware"**: Andrew Newberg, MD, and Mark Robert Waldman, *How God Changes Your Brain: Breakthrough Findings from a Leading Neuroscientist* (Ballantine, 2009), pp. 48–52.

135 **"Pastors can also expand"**: Ibid., pp. 52–54.

135 **"Other research on brain chemistry"**: The Center for Neuroeconomic Studies at Claremont Graduate University has identified this connection. Researchers there aspire to learn more about whether certain conditions can enhance production of oxytocin. See www.neuroeconomicstudies.org.

138 **"The goal was always"**: Owen Chadwick, *Western Asceticism: Selected Translations with Introduction and Notes,* (Library of Christian Classics, Westminster Press, 1958), p. 22.

139 **"Americans have become suspicious"**: Wuthnow, *After Heaven*, p. 112. Based on Wuthnow's extensive research (including surveys and interviews), he writes: "Contrary to the maxim, 'No pain, no gain,' many Americans seem in fact to be skeptical of anything that has to be achieved at too great a cost."

140 **"They're far more observant"**: James P. Gannon, "Is God Dead in Europe?" *USA Today*, January 8, 2006.

144 **"Certain strains of feminism"**: Rita Nakishima Brock and Rebecca Ann Parker express concern about Christianity's traditional

reverence for sacrifice in the essay "Can Sacrifice Save?" See http://www.uuworld.org/2002/02/feature1a.html.

CHAPTER SIX

157 **"The community exemplifies 'New Monasticism'":** For more on New Monasticism, see Jonathan Wilson-Hartgrove's *New Monasticism: What It Has to Say to Today's Church—An Insider's Perspective* (Brazos Press, 2008) or www.newmonasticism.org.

168 **"Similar successes arose":** Eagle Brook has recently discontinued group spiritual direction. The church now offers spiritual direction on an individual basis.

169 **"Rather, the one called is continually acting in the world":** Mark Tranvik, director of the Lilly Endowment Grant on Vocation at Augsburg College, spells out the role of community in vocation on page 6 of his unpublished paper, "Vocation at Augsburg College."

178 **"This blunts the argument":** Churches grow enormously when they give similar people a place to gather in homogenous clusters, according to a theory developed by Donald McGavran and explained in Bill Bishop's *The Big Sort: Why the Clustering of Like-Minded America Is Tearing Us Apart* (Houghton Mifflin, 2008). Bishop tells how contemporary pastors of fast-growing congregations have built on the methods that McGavran deduced in the practices of J. Waskom

EPILOGUE: FIXING THE IMMINENT FUTURE

184 **"Redemption, for instance, doesn't seem to count":** Fallen public figures who resigned rather than try to claim redemption before an unforgiving public include Senator Larry Craig (a

Republican from Idaho), Obama advisers Van Jones and Saman-
tha Power, and Hillary Clinton adviser Geraldine Ferraro.

185 **"Fundraisers increasingly try to make":** Examples of the movement to make giving painless include iGive.com, goodsearch.com,
and nonprofitshoppingmall.com. These sites make giving as easy
as shopping or searching the Web. Another example would be
"green" credit cards from Bank of America and Wells Fargo,
which let users earn points that can be redeemed for donations to
eco-friendly organizations. No sacrifice necessary.

189 **"The Southern Presbyterian Church went so far as to declare in
1864":** Paul Johnson, *A History of Christianity* (Simon & Schuster, 1976), p. 438.

SUGGESTED READING
FROM THE AUTHOR

Bader-Saye, Scott. *Following Jesus in a Culture of Fear* (Brazos Press, 2007)
Theologian Scott Bader-Saye recognizes how fear has become pervasive in American culture and how it hinders authentic discipleship. Readers will likely find his distinctions helpful in sorting out how to be both prudent and courageous in response to the Gospel.

Bishop, Bill. *The Big Sort: Why the Clustering of Like-Minded America Is Tearing Us Apart* (Houghton Mifflin, 2008)
From reams of sociological data, journalist Bill Bishop tells the unsettling story of our recent tendency as Americans to settle in ideological enclaves. He includes a chapter on religious clustering. He also unpacks why it matters on a profound level that Americans, whether they lean liberal or conservative, increasingly steer clear of those who might question their ideas and beliefs.

Bonheoffer, Dietrich. *Discipleship* (Fortress Press, 2003)
Dietrich Bonheoffer has no time for platitudes. Readers hungry to know where the life of faith leads find a refreshingly honest guide in this classic from a theological genius and twentieth-century martyr. That the title has recently been changed from *The Cost of Discipleship* to simply *Discipleship* marks a richly ironic sign of our times, but the text is as powerful and relevant as ever.

Bonheoffer, Dietrich. *Life Together: The Classic Exploration of Faith in Community* (HarperOne, 1978)
In this short and accessibly written book, Bonheoffer helps Christians understand how churches are unique among institutions. Deep

awareness of sin and forgiveness enables a unique type of love—for one another and for the world at large—to emerge. Every churchgoer should read it.

Hudnut-Buemler, James. *In Pursuit of the Almighty's Dollar: A History of Money and American Protestantism* (University of North Carolina Press, 2007)

This book may be a bit wonky, but I found it fascinating. A disciplined historian treats the how and why of church fundraising as lenses for understanding major themes in American religious history. Readers with patience for detail will learn a lot by following the money.

Kenneson, Philip D. & Street, James L. *Selling Out the Church: The Dangers of Church Marketing* (Wipf & Stock, 2003)

Two theologians carefully challenge the widely held assumption that says churches need to master the art of corporate-style marketing. Their thoughtful analysis considers the implicit risks to church integrity and spiritual formation when churches travel the road of trying to entice and delight. Their proposed solutions differ from my own and helpfully enrich the dialogue.

Livermore, David A. *Serving with Eyes Wide Open: Doing Short-Term Missions with Cultural Intelligence* (Baker Books, 2006)

David Livermore appreciates from an evangelical perspective how short-term mission trips are too often framed to satisfy the desires of missionaries. This book analyzes common problems in this area of church life and offers practical insights for congregations that want to do better.

Wilson-Hartgrove, Jonathan. *New Monasticism: What It Has to Say to Today's Church—An Insider's Perspective* (Brazos Press, 2008)

"New monastics," such as members of Abbey Way Covenant Church in Minneapolis, have established dozens of communities in the United States and abroad. By and large, they commit to live together in communities marked by intentional practices, such as eating, praying, sharing resources and serving the needy. Their motivations and practices help stoke imagination about what's possible in terms of living an authentic Christian life in 21st century America.

INDEX

Clergy (*continued*)
  disillusioned, 16
  establishment of, 208n
  example of, 191
  exodus of, 199n
  guidance of, 79
  homosexual, 101
  laity empowered by, 25, 129, 135
  marriage among, 7
  overweight, 93
  sway held by, 13
  training of, 71
  women leading, 21
  worship created by, 14
Clinton, Hillary, 59–60
Cloister, 157
Comfort, 172
  congregation's, 134
  sermons that, 80
the Comforter. *See* Holy Spirit
Commandments
  modern interpretation of, 49
  tenth, 95
  violation of, xv
Commitment, 172
  charity, 172
  church, 113
  mutual, 41
  prayer, 90
  public profession of, 45
Common good, 190
Communion, 17, 186
  policy, 84
  sacrament of, 82
  table, 120
Community, 149, 161
  believers making, xvii
  Christian, xi

Church, ix, 61, 122, 181
  defining, 156
  Evangelical, 30
  examples of, 133
  gated, 185
  hope in, 173
  Jesus Christ in, 159
  larger, 169
  leaving, 208n
  levels of, 163
  local, 52
  narrowly defined, 106
  needs, 174
  outcasts, 166
  outreach, 176
  pioneering, 158
  resources, 186
  role of, 210n
  service, 175
  small-group, 154
  vision, 35
  weak, 63
  worship, 105
Compassion, 173, 185
  difficult, 54
  expanding, 131
  expanding of, 135
  image of, 132
  missionary, 171
  parental, 136
  teen, 174
Competition, 189
  congregational, 28
  soul, 27
Confession, 159
  amends through, 83
  mood of, 40
  sin, 39, 66